# Cognitive
# Development

---

## Its Cultural and
## Social Foundations

# Cognitive Development

## Its Cultural and Social Foundations

### A. R. LURIA

TRANSLATED BY
Martin Lopez-Morillas and Lynn Solotaroff

EDITED BY
Michael Cole

HARVARD UNIVERSITY PRESS
CAMBRIDGE, MASSACHUSETTS
AND LONDON, ENGLAND
1976

Library of Congress Cataloging in Publication Data

Luriia, Aleksandr Romanovich, 1902-
  Cognitive development, its cultural and social
foundations.

  Translation of Ob istoricheskom razvitii poznavatel'nykh
protsessov.
  Bibliography: p.
  Includes index.
  1. Cognition. 2. Personality and culture.
3. Acculturation, 3. Vygotsky, Lev Semenovich,
1896-1934.    I. Title
BF311.L8713            153.7            76-24817
ISBN 0-674-13731-0

# Preface

The history of this book is somewhat unusual. All of its observational material was collected in 1931-32, during the Soviet Union's most radical restructuring: the elimination of illiteracy, the transition to a collectivist economy, and the readjustment of life to new socialist principles. This period offered a unique opportunity to observe how decisively all these reforms effected not only a broadening of outlook but also radical changes in the structure of cognitive processes.

The Marxist-Leninist thesis that all fundamental human cognitive activities take shape in a matrix of social history and form the products of sociohistorical development was amplified by L. S. Vygotsky to serve as the basis of a great deal of Soviet psychological research. None of the investigations, however, was sufficiently complete or comprehensive to verify these assumptions directly. The experimental program described in this book was conceived in response to this situation, and at Vygotsky's suggestion.

We did our research in the remoter regions of Uzbekistan and Kirghizia, in the *kishlaks* (villages) and *dzhailaus* (mountain pasturelands) of the country. Our efforts could have met with equal success, however, in the remoter areas of European Russia, among the peoples of the North, or in the nomad camps of the Siberian Northeast. Despite the high levels of creativity in science, art, and architecture attained in the ancient culture of Uzbekistan, the masses had lived for centuries in economic stagnation and illiteracy, their development hindered among other things by the religion of Islam. Only the radical restructuring of the economy, the rapid elimination of illiteracy, and the removal of the Moslem influence could achieve, over and above an expansion in world view, a genuine revolution in cognitive activity.

Our data indicate the decisive changes that can occur in going from graphic and functional—concrete and practical—methods of thinking to much more theoretical and abstract modes brought about by fundamental changes in social conditions, in this instance by the socialist transformation of an entire culture. Thus the experimental observations shed light on one aspect of human cognitive activity that has received little scientific study but that corroborates the dialectics of social development.

Today I know full well that certain advances in the collection of psychological data could provide more modern research with greater methodological sophistication and a more adequate conceptual system. But the uniqueness of the profound and rapid social changes taking place while these observations were made justifies me, I believe, in publishing this research in the form in which it was collected.

This book stands in contrast to a large number of "culturalogical" studies made outside the USSR in the 1940s and 1950s. Some of them, by reactionary authors, try to apply "racial" theories to the data in order to prove the subjects' "inferiority." Other studies limit themselves to describing differences in the cognitive processes found in "backward" cultures, frequently referring only to these people's narrower world view, without probing the specific characteristics of the psychological structure of their cognitive activity, without linking such features to the basic forms of social life, and, needless to say, without following the rapid and fundamental changes that occur when such forms are radically restructured (attempting instead only to adapt these people to "Western culture").

I am fully aware that the various chapters in the book are set forth unevenly; some details are treated adequately, others only outlined. The reason for publishing all the chapters, however, is to provide an impetus for further research in this field.

I am deeply indebted to my teacher and friend L. S. Vygotsky (who died shortly after this work was completed) as well as to several participants in the two investigatory expeditions to central Asia, among them, P. I. Leventuev, F. N. Shemyakin, A. Bagautdinov, E. Baiburov, L. S. Gazaryants, V. V. Zakharova, E. I. Mordkovich, K. Khakimov, and M. Khodzhinova.

A.R.L.

Moscow
1976

# Contents

# Foreword

MICHAEL COLE

In order to appreciate this remarkable book more fully, the reader may find it helpful to have some idea of the intellectual and social climate at the time when Alexander Luria, still a young man, set out for Central Asia. In 1921 he completed his undergraduate work at the university in his native town of Kazan. After graduating from the humanities faculty (there was still no psychology department as such at the time), Luria entered the Kazan medical school. His interest in psychology interrupted his medical studies, however, and in 1923 he accepted a position at the Institute of Psychology at Moscow University.

Luria arrived at the institute during a period of great ferment. In psychology, as in many areas of Russian intellectual life, there were many different ideas about how things should change following the revolution. The prerevolutionary director of the institute, G. T. Chelpanov, had been replaced by K. N. Kornilov, who undertook to remold psychology along Marxist lines. But there was no firm agreement on exactly what a Marxist psychology should look like.

Kornilov himself tried to set up guidelines for a Marxist psychology in his *Textbook of Psychology from the Standpoint of Materialism,* first published in 1926 and later reprinted several times. His major theme was the inadequacy of the phenomenological psychology then holding sway in Russia and in Europe generally. In his emphasis on simple reactions, and the accurate measurement of their speed, form, and duration, his "reactological" school of psychology bore many similarities to American behaviorism, then coming into prominence. On his arrival in Moscow Luria himself had been more influenced by events in Germany than those in America. He had read the early work of the Gestalt psychologists, and had even written a small essay attempting to unify certain Freudian ideas with an objective research methodology. (The fruits of this work appeared much later in English under the title *The Nature of Human Conflicts.*)

In 1923 Luria met Lev Vygotsky at a conference in Leningrad. Vygotsky was invited to work in Moscow in 1924, and thus began the collaboration leading to the research described in this book. Vygotsky believed that psychology in the mid-1920s was in a state of crisis, which had, in effect, split the field into two disjoint subdisciplines. On the one hand, the work of Sechenov, Pavlov, and other natural scientists had succeeded in establishing a material basis for *elementary* psychological processes. But the reflex approach provided no adequate method for dealing with the *complex* psychological functions that traditionally formed another chief concern of psychology—voluntary memory, abstract problem solving, and creative imagination, for example. On the other hand, psychologists who took these complex functions as their subject matter found themselves confined to verbal description based solely on introspection, a procedure that did not satisfy Soviet scholars' desire for an objective, materialist psychology.

Both Vygotsky and Luria accepted the principle that all psychological processes have a basis in reflexes. However, they resisted the position, popular in America at the time (and accepted by Kornilov), that complex psychological processes can be *reduced* to chains of reflexes. Vygotsky sought the proper minimal unit of a new cognitive psychology which retained the basic characteristics of uniquely human psychological processes.

The elementary feature characteristic of human consciousness chosen by Vygotsky was *mediation*. According to this conception, first put forth by Vygotsky in the early 1920s, the behavior of both animals and man is built upon a reflex base. But man is not restricted to simple stimulus-response reflexes; he is able to make indirect connections between incoming stimulation and his responses through various mediating links. When man introduces a change in the environment through his own behavior, these very changes influence his later behavior. The simple reflex is changed into a reflex system in which the tools a man uses to influence his environment become signs that he then uses to influence his own behavior as well. Vygotsky believed that this formulation allowed him to retain the principle of the material reflex as the basis of behavior, and also to analyze human psychological functions as instances of complex, mediated, mental acts.

This line of theorizing has become familiar in the United States through several publications by Vygotsky (1962) and Luria (1961). They apply the concept of mediation almost exclusively to the development of mental processes in children, especially to the role of language in development. Vygotsky and Luria stressed that mental development must be viewed as a historical process in which the child's social and nonsocial environment induces the development of mediating processes and the various higher mental functions. "Historical" in the context of child development has generally been interpreted as an individual phenomenon, although Luria has always emphasized that word meanings provide the child with the distilled results of the history of his society.

This book is concerned with the historical aspect of mental development in a quite different sense. In 1930, Luria and Vygotsky published a monograph entitled "Essays in the History of Behavior." This work raised the possibility that the principles they had been applying to individual development might have parallels in sociocultural development as well. Clear examples of external mediation were seen in such phenomena as the use of knotted ropes to aid memory among tribes in South America or the ritual sticks discovered among aborigines in Australia.

Such data were of course only anecdotal at best, but they received a good deal of attention in Soviet social science at the time. It is probably no coincidence that an edited version of two of Lévy-Bruhl's books on primitive thought processes appeared in 1930. Although the editors of the book expressed doubts about some of Lévy-Bruhl's formulations, in general they accepted his view that social changes were accompanied by fundamental changes in thought processes.

At this same time, as Luria tells us in his preface to this book, enormous social changes were taking place in all parts of the USSR.

The campaign to bring collectivized agricultural practices to the entire country was in full swing. For the peasants of central Asia, the new order indeed required monumental changes in age-old cultural patterns.

Thus, in search of support for their new psychological theory as well as evidence of the intellectual benefits of the new socialist order, Luria set out for central Asia. Vygotsky, already ill with tuberculosis (he died in 1934), could only learn of these journeys second hand.

After two expeditions during which the data in this book were gathered, Luria made some preliminary public descriptions of his results, but the intellectual climate in Moscow at the time was not at all friendly to his conclusions. Although Luria clearly emphasized the beneficial consequences of collectivization, critics pointed out that his data could be read as an insult to the people with whom he had been working (Razmyslov, 1934). The status of national minorities in the USSR has long been a sensitive issue (not unlike the issue of ethnic minorities in the United States). It was all well and good to show that uneducated, traditional peasants quickly learned the modes of thought characteristic of industrialized, socialist peoples, but it was definitely not acceptable to say anything that could be interpreted as negative about these people at a time when their participation in national life was still so tenuous.

By 1974, when this book was published in the USSR, there was greater readiness to consider the implications of different patterns of intellectual behavior characteristic of different social groups. L. I. Antsyferova, a leading Soviet theoretician, has summarized the contribution of the book: "A. Luria's book is an important and, it may be said without exaggeration, a unique contribution to the methodology and theory of psychological science and to the development of its basic principle of historicism" (Antsyferova, 1976, p. 256).

Part of the initial controversy over Luria's cross-cultural work may have arisen from the developmental orientation he brought to this topic. His general purpose was to show the sociohistorical roots of all basic cognitive processes; the structure of thought depends upon the structure of the dominant types of activity in different cultures. From this set of assumptions, it follows that practical thinking will predominate in societies that are characterized by practical manipulations of objects, and more "abstract" forms of "theoretical" activity in technological societies will induce more abstract, theoretical thinking. The parallel between individual and social development produces a strong proclivity to interpret all behavioral differences in developmental terms. Paradoxically, it is exactly this orientation, together with Luria's genius at using what he calls the "clinical method," that makes this book so relevant today.

Luria conducted his research before cross-cultural psychology became an accepted discipline in Europe and America. There is now a rather large and growing literature on the questions raised in this book (see Berry and Dasen, 1974; Cole and Scribner, 1974; or Lloyd, 1972, for summaries). But we have yet to resolve ambiguities in the interpretation of cultural differences of the kind Luria so clearly documents.

Luria's style of interpreting these data is similar to the tradition that attributes performance differences between groups in two cultures to the same processes that give rise to performance differences between younger and older children within the same culture. This line of interpretation has an honorable history, as shown in the work of Greenfield and Bruner (1966) and work carried out in the Piagetian tradition (Dasen, 1972). Within this framework, Luria's data are unique in showing very sharp changes among adults exposed to different work contexts and to minimal levels of education (although some data of a similar nature have been obtained by Scribner, 1974).

My own interpretation of such data is somewhat different, since I am skeptical of the usefulness of applying developmental theories cross-culturally. Thus, what Luria interprets as the acquisition of new modes of thought, I am more inclined to interpret as changes in the application of previously available modes to the particular problems and contexts of discourse represented by the experimental setting. But the value of this book does not hinge on our interpretation of Luria's results. As he emphasizes at several points, this text represents an extended pilot project that can never be repeated. It will be for other investigators, working in those parts of the world where traditional societies still exist, to iron out the interpretation of such findings.

It is not only the uniqueness of the historical circumstances that makes this work of contemporary interest. To my knowledge, there is not one example in the cross-cultural literature of the application of the methods used here. Luria is simply a brilliant craftsman in his use of the clinical method to explore the reasoning processes that his subjects bring to bear on the problems he poses. His carefully guided probing, his use of the hypothetical opponent ("but one man told me . . ."), the inclusion of several people whose arguments among themselves become his data, have no parallel in the psychological investigations of our century.

Enough said. Luria's informants say it better. Unless you have seen it for yourself, it is better not to comment.

## REFERENCES

Antsyferova, L. I. Review of A. R. Luria's The historical development of mental processes. *Social Sciences,* 1976, *7,* 254-256.

Berry, J. W., and P. R. Dasen, eds. *Culture and cognition.* London: Methuen, 1973

Cole, M., and S. Scribner. *Culture and thought.* New York: Wiley, 1974.

Dasen, P. R. Cross-cultural Piagetian research: A summary. *Journal of Cross-cultural Psychology,* 1972, *3,* 23-39.

Greenfield, P. M., and J. S. Bruner. Culture and cognitive growth. *International Journal of Psychology,* 1966, *1,* 89-107.

Kornilov, K. N. *Textbook of psychology from the standpoint of materialism.* Moscow: State Publishing House, 1926.

Lévy-Bruhl, L. *Primitive mentality.* Moscow: Atheist Publishing House, 1930 (in Russian).

Lloyd, B. B. *Perception and cognition: A cross-cultural perspective.* Harmondsworth: Penguin Books, 1972.

Luria, A. R. *The nature of human conflicts.* New York: Liveright, 1932.

_____ *The role of speech in the regulation of normal and abnormal behavior.* London: Pergamon Press, 1961.

Razmyslov, P. Vygotsky and Luria's cultural-historical theory of psychology. *Knigii proletarskii revolutsii,* 1934, *4,* 78-86 (in Russian).

Scribner, S. Developmental aspects of categorized recall in a West African society. *Cognitive Psychology,* 1974, *6,* 475-494.

Vygotsky, L. S. *Thought and language.* Cambridge: Massachusetts Institute of Technology Press, 1962.

_____ and A. R. Luria. *Essays in the history of behavior.* Moscow-Leningrad: State Publishing House, 1930 (in Russian).

# Cognitive Development

---

## Its Cultural and Social Foundations

# 1

## The Problem

It seems surprising that the science of psychology has avoided the idea that many mental processes are social and historical in origin, or that important manifestations of human consciousness have been directly shaped by the basic practices of human activity and the actual forms of culture.

Beginning in the middle of the nineteenth century, psychology tried to view itself as an independent science aspiring to an objective analysis of the physiological mechanisms involved in behavior. At various points in its development, psychology distinguished several basic mechanisms behind mental processes. During the middle of the nineteenth century, attention was focused on the principles of association, which were supposed to make up the whole fabric of human mental life. Toward the second half of the century, some investigators turned their attention to more complex mental phenomena. Wilhelm Wundt, the founder of psychology as a natural science, called these mental events "active apperceptions." At the turn of the century, most psychologists assumed that these mental "acts" and "functions" underlay all forms of thinking and willing. The Würzburg school exemplified this new trend in psychology.

But scientific psychology soon proved itself inadequate to the task of investigating every facet of active mental life. Consequently, one branch of psychology set itself up as an independent discipline concerned with more complex mental phenomena; this new school was closely linked to the neo-Kantian idealism supported by Cassirer's "philosophy of symbolic forms."

The breakaway of the study of complex mental processes provoked a strong reaction among the psychologists in the natural-science tradition. During the first decade of the twentieth century, both Gestalt psychology in Germany and behaviorism in the United States took on the scientific study of the most complex and integral forms of mental activity as well as the more elementary ones. Gestalt psychology, largely restricting itself to the established natural-science psychology, tried to do away with the atomism and associationism typical of traditional psychology, and to discover the integral structural laws found most clearly in perception and perhaps in other psychological processes. American behaviorism saw a way out of the difficulties in traditional psychology by refusing to study the subjective world and by trying to find natural-science laws of integral behavior. This approach rested on a behavioral analysis developed by physiologists studying higher nervous processes.

During the course, however, of psychology's attempt to make itself an exact science, it has looked for laws of mental activity "within the organism." It has regarded association, or apperception, the structural nature of perception, or conditioned reflexes underlying behavior as either natural and unchanging properties of the organism (physiological psychology) or as manifestations or intrinsic properties of the mind (idealistic psychology). The notion that the intrinsic properties and laws of mental activity remain unchanging has also led to attempts to set up a positivist social psychology and sociology based on the premise that social activities display mental properties operating within individuals. Wundt devoted the second half of his life to his multivolume *Völkerpsychologie* (Folk Psychology), in which he attempted to decipher social phenomena such as religion, myths, morals, and law from the viewpoint of the psychology of the individual human being. For Wundt, these aspects of social behavior displayed the same natural laws of individual association and apperception. The numerous attempts to find the instincts of the individual at the bottom of all social phenomena (beginning with McDougall and continuing on to the modern neo-Freudians and ethologists who regard war as the result of innate aggressive impulses in the individual) have only continued this trend.

We cannot doubt that scientific psychology made considerable progress during the past century and contributed greatly to our knowledge of mental activity. Nonetheless, it has generally ignored the social origin of higher mental processes. The patterns it describes turn out to be the same for animals and for human beings, for humans of different cultures and different historical eras, and for elementary mental processes and complex forms of mental activity.

Moreover, the laws of logical thought, active remembering, selective attention, and acts of the will in general, which form the basis for the most complex and characteristic higher forms of human mental activity, successfully resisted causal interpretation, and thus remained beyond the forefront of the progression of scientific thought.

It was not by accident that Bergson spoke of the laws of "memory of the spirit" in addition to the natural laws of "memory of the body," while neo-Kantian philosophers distinguished (in addition to the laws of association that could be analyzed by natural science) laws of "symbolic forms" which functioned as manifestations of the "spiritual world" and had neither an origin nor a theory: they could be described but not accounted for. Despite objective progress, therefore, a major field of knowledge remained divorced from causal explanations, and could not be studied in any meaningful way. This situation called for decisive steps to reexamine the basic approaches to mental activity in order to make psychology a truly scientific discipline decisively rejecting any kind of dualism and thus opening the way for a causal analysis of even the most complex mental phenomena. This reexamination implied the abandonment of subjectivism in psychology and the treatment of human consciousness as a product of social history.

## THE SOCIOHISTORICAL EVOLUTION OF THE MIND

The first attempts to approach human mental processes as the products of evolution were taken in the second half of the nineteenth century by Charles Darwin and his successor Herbert Spencer. These scientists attempted to trace the ways in which complex forms of mental activity develop and how elementary forms of biological adaptation to environmental conditions become more complex through the evolutionary process. The evolutionary approach, which was quite valid for a comparative study of mental development in the animal world, found itself in something of a blind alley when it tried to study the evolution of human mental activity. Notions about individual development reproducing the development of the species (the "biogenetic law" or the "law of recapitulation"), which became widespread in their day, clearly produced little and yielded only superficial and reactionary conclusions, for example that the thought processes of primitive peoples closely resemble those of children (Tylor, 1874) and indicate the "racial inferiority" of backward peoples.

As early as the beginning of the present century, Durkheim assumed that the basic processes of the mind are not manifestations of the spirit's inner life or the result of natural evolution, but rather originated in society (Durkheim and Mauss, 1963). Durkheim's ideas formed the basis for a number of other studies, in which the French psychologist Pierre Janet and others played a prominent part.

Janet proposed that complex forms of memory, as well as complex ideas of space, time, and number, had their source in the concrete history of society rather than in any intrinsic categories of spiritual life. In Janet's opinion, uncontrolled remembering and return to the past, which Bergson regarded as the most typical manifestation of the "memory of the spirit," have their roots in the storage and transfer of information in primitive society, in particular, in "messenger" activity, a function of a particular individual in primitive societies—someone who used special mnemonic techniques.

Classical idealistic psychology regarded notions of space and time as irreducible products of consciousness. But with considerable justification the French psychologists asserted that the basic conceptual categories of space originated not in biology but in society, going back to the spatial arrangement of the primitive nomad camp. The Frenchmen reasoned similarly in their search for the origin of the concept of time in the conditions of primitive society and its means for reckoning time. They also looked for a similar explanation of the origin of the concept of number.

The French school of sociology, however, had one major shortcoming that invalidated its theories. It refused to interpret the influence of society on the individual mind as the influence of the socioeco-

nomic system and the actual forms of social activity on individual consciousness. Unlike the approach of historical materialism, the French
school considered this process only as an interaction between "collective representations" or "social consciousness" and individual consciousness, all the while paying no attention to particular social systems, histories, or practices. By approaching the relations between
labor and production as individual activities, Durkheim regarded society as the sphere of collective representations and convictions shaping
the mental life of the individual. Such was the point of departure for
Durkheim's subsequent work, as well as that of the entire French
school of sociology (Blondel, 1922; Durkheim and Mauss, 1963; and
others).

The French school thus side-tracked both particular forms of work
and the economic conditions forming the basis of all social life. It
described the formation of the individual mind as a purely spiritual
event occurring in isolation from concrete practice and the particular
conditions of its physical milieu. For this reason, the French school's
attempts to trace the distinctive features of the human mind at various
stages of historical development led to conclusions that held back the
creation of a truly materialistic psychology.

The work of Lucien Lévy-Bruhl (1930), a representative of the
French school, was highly influential. From his assumption that human thinking in a primitive culture is produced by "collective representations" predominant in the society, Lévy-Bruhl concluded that
primitive thought follows its own laws: it is "prelogical," loosely
organized, and operates by the "law of participation." Thus he believed that primitive thought was magical, reflecting the belief systems
and primitive magic rather than the practical relations between human
beings and reality.

Lévy-Bruhl was the first to point out the qualitative features of
primitive thought and the first to treat logical processes as products of
historical development. He had a great influence on psychologists in
the 1920s who tried to go beyond simplistic notions about the mind as
a by-product of natural selection and to understand human consciousness as a product of sociohistorical development. Their analysis, however, cut off human thought in its earlier stages of historical development from actual activity and cognitive processes, which were then
treated as the result of beliefs; if primitive people really did think ac-

cording to the laws set forth by Lévy-Bruhl, they would scarcely have survived for a single day.

The opponents of Lévy-Bruhl relied on experimental data (Rivers, 1926; Leroy, 1927), and allied themselves with anthropologists and linguists such as George Boas (1911). In challenging Lévy-Bruhl's findings, they proposed that the intellectual apparatus of humans in primitive cultures was fundamentally identical to that of more advanced people. They even suggested that his own findings indicate that people living in primitive conditions think in accordance with the same logical laws that we ourselves do. The only basic difference in thinking is that they generalize the facts of the external world into different categories from those we are accustomed to use (Rivers, 1926). Their thinking reflects neither racial inferiority nor differences in beliefs. It becomes intelligible to us, however, only if we understand the people's actual living conditions and the language they use (Boas, 1911). This was the approach to human mental processes at the time that our work began.

The research reported here, undertaken forty years ago under Vygotsky's initiative and in the context of unprecedented social and cultural change, took the view that higher cognitive activities remain sociohistorical in nature, and that the structure of mental activity—not just the specific content but also the general forms basic to all cognitive processes—change in the course of historical development. For this reason our research remains valuable even today.

### Initial Assumptions

Soviet psychology, using the notion of consciousness as "conscious existence" (*das bewusste Sein*) as a starting point, has rejected the view that consciousness represents an "intrinsic property of mental life," invariably present in every mental state and independent of historical development. In line with Marx and Lenin, Soviet psychology maintains that consciousness is the highest form of reflection of reality; it is, moreover, not given in advance, unchanging and passive, but shaped by activity and used by human beings to orient themselves to their environment, not only in adapting to conditions but in restructuring them.

It has become a basic principle of materialistic psychology that mental processes depend on active life forms in an appropriate environment. Such a psychology also assumes that human action changes the environment so that human mental life is a product of continually *new* activities manifest in social practice.

The way in which the historically established forms of human mental life correlate with reality has come to depend more and more on complex social practices. The tools that human beings in society use to manipulate that environment, as well as the products of previous generations which help shape the mind of the growing child, also affect these mental forms. In his development, the child's first social relations and his first exposure to a linguistic system (of special significance) determine the forms of his mental activity. All these environmental factors are decisive for the sociohistorical development of consciousness. New motives for action appear under extremely complex patterns of social practice. Thus are created new problems, new modes of behavior, new methods of taking in information, and new systems of reflecting reality.

From the outset, the social forms of human life begin to determine human mental development. Consider the development of conscious activity in children. From birth on, children live in a world of things social labor has created: products of history. They learn to communicate with others around them and develop relationships with things through the help of adults. Children assimilate language—a ready-made product of sociohistorical development—and use it to analyze, generalize, and encode experience. They name things, denoting them with expressions established earlier in human history, and thus assign things to certain categories and acquire knowledge. Once a child calls something a "watch" (*chasy*), he immediately incorporates it into a system of things related to time (*chas*); once he calls a moving object a "steamship" (*parovoz*), he automatically isolates its defining properties—motion (*vozit'*) by means of "steam" (*par*). Language, which mediates human perception, results in extremely complex operations: the analysis and synthesis of incoming information, the perceptual ordering of the world, and the encoding of impressions into systems. Thus words—the basic linguistic units—carry not only meaning but also the fundamental units of consciousness reflecting the external world.

But the world of particular objects and verbal meanings that humans receive from earlier generations organizes not just perception and memory (thus ensuring the assimilation of experiences common to all humankind); it also establishes some important conditions for later, more complex developments in consciousness. Men can deal even with "absent" objects, and so "duplicate the world," through words, which maintain the system of meanings whether or not the person is directly experiencing the objects the words refer to. Hence a new source of productive imagination arises: it can reproduce objects as well as reorder their relationships and thus serve as the basis for highly complex creative processes. Men use a complex system of syntactical relations among the individual words in sentences, and are then able to formulate complex relationships among entities, and to generate and transmit thoughts and opinions. Because of the hierarchical system of individual sentences, of which verbal and logical constructions are a typical example, humans have at their disposal a powerful objective tool that permits them not only to reflect individual objects or situations but to create objective logical codes. Such codes enable a person to go beyond direct experience and to draw conclusions that have the same objectivity as the data of direct sensory experience. In other words, social history has established the system of language and logical codes that permit men to make the leap from the sensory to the rational; for the founders of materialistic philosophy, this transition was as important as that from nonliving to living matter.

Human consciousness thus ceases to be an "intrinsic quality of the human spirit" with no history or intractibility to causal analysis. We begin to understand it as the highest form of reflection of reality that sociohistorical development creates: a system of objectively existing agents gives birth to it and causal historical analysis makes it accessible to us.

The views expressed here are important not merely because they deal with human consciousness as a product of social history and point the way to a scientific historical analysis; they are also important because they deal with the process of broadening the limits of consciousness and of creating codes as a result of human social life. Moreover, some mental processes cannot develop apart from the appropriate forms of social life. This last observation is decisive for psychology and has opened up new and unforeseen prospects.

In learning complex activities with objects, undergoing correction of their own behavior through social relations, and in mastering complex linguistic systems, children are invariably led to develop new motives and forms of conscious activity, and to pose new problems. The child replaces his earlier manipulative games with others involving new roles and plots. There then appear socially conditioned rules for these games and these become rules for behavior.

Under the influence of adult speech, the child distinguishes and fixes on behavioral goals; he rethinks relationships between things; he thinks up new forms of child-adult relations; he reevaluates the behavior of others and then his own; he develops new emotional responses and affective categories which through language become generalized emotions and character traits. This entire complex process, which is closely related to the incorporation of language into the child's mental life, results in a radical reorganization of the thinking that provides for the reflection of reality and the very processes of human activity.

The very young child perceiving an unfamiliar object does not name it; he uses different mental processes from an adolescent who has mastered language and thus analyzes incoming information with the aid of verbal meanings. A child who develops habits by drawing conclusions from immediate personal experience uses different mental devices from an adolescent who mediates each behavioral act through norms established by social experience. The direct impressions that dominate the young child give way in the adolescent to the omnipresent abstractions and generalizations of external and internal speech.

In his analysis of the fundamental developmental changes in mental processes (changes expressing successive forms of reflection of reality), Vygotsky observed that although the young child thinks by remembering, an adolescent remembers by thinking. Thus the formation of complex forms of the reflection of reality and activity goes hand in hand with radical changes in the mental processes that affect these forms of reflection and underlie activity. Vygotsky called this thesis the semantic and system structure of consciousness.

Now the psychologist can not only describe the different and changing forms of conscious life of both the child and the adult; he can also analyze changes in the structure of those mental processes underlying mental activity at different stages of development and discover the hitherto unsuspected changes in their "interfunctional relationships." He can thus trace the historical development of mental systems.

In the early years of Soviet psychology, investigators paid most attention to changes in the mental development of children. In the past half century brilliant discoveries have drastically altered the basic theoretical concepts of psychology: Vygotsky's description of the development of word meanings; Leontiev's analysis of developmental changes in the child's organization of reality; Zaporozhets' (1960) description of the formation of complex voluntary actions; and Galperin's (1957) and Elkonin's (1960) investigations of the formation of internalized "mental actions." In spite of these profound shifts and recent alterations in its profile, psychology has barely begun to study the specific sociohistorical shaping of mental processes. We still do not know whether changes in sociohistorical structures or changes in the nature of social practice result only in broadened experience, acquisition of new habits and knowledge, literacy, and so forth, or whether they result in radical reorganization of mental processes, changes at the structural level of mental activity, and the formation of new mental systems. Proof of the latter would be of fundamental significance for psychology as a science of social history.

Psychology has made few attempts to deal with this problem, partly because of the infrequency of occasions when an investigator can observe how the restructuring of social systems has brought about rapidly changing forms of social life and rapidly shifting forms of consciousness; partly because many students of "backward" peoples have tried—either consciously or unconsciously—to justify the existing inequalities.

Our research took place during a period of rapid and fundamental reorganization of social structures. Hence we could observe the sociohistorical shaping of mental processes, and thus could close up a major gap in the science of psychology.

## THE RESEARCH SITUATION

The aim of our research—an analysis of the sociohistorical shaping of mental processes—determined the choice of the conditions for obtaining the best results. These conditions existed at the beginning of the 1930s in remote parts of the Soviet Union. In the late 1920s and early 1930s, these regions witnessed a radical restructuring of their socioeconomic system and culture.

Before the revolution, the people of Uzbekistan lived in a backward economy based mainly on the raising of cotton. The *kishlak* (village) dwellers displayed remnants of a once-high culture together with virtually complete illiteracy, and also showed the pronounced influence of the Islamic religion.

When the socialist revolution eliminated dominance and submission as class relations, people oppressed one day enjoyed a free existence the next. And for the first time, they experienced responsibility for their own future. Uzbekistan became a republic with collective agricultural production; industry also began to develop. The appearance of a new economic system brought with it new forms of social activity: the collective evaluation of work plans, the recognition and correction of shortcomings, and the allocation of economic functions. Naturally the socioeconomic life of these regions underwent a complete transformation. The radical changes in social class structure were accompanied by new cultural shifts.

An extensive network of schools opened up in outlying areas that had been virtually 100 percent illiterate for centuries. Despite their short-term nature, the literacy programs familiarized large numbers of adults with the elements of modern technology. Adults in school took time out from their everyday activities and began to master elements of simple but "theoretical" pursuits. In acquiring the rudiments of reading and writing, people had to break down spoken language into its constituents and encode it in a system of symbols. They mastered the concept of number, which had been used only in practical activities, but now became an abstract entity to be learned for its own sake. As a result, people became acquainted not only with new fields of knowledge but also with *new motives for action*.

Many other specialized short-term courses were introduced, most importantly in preschool education and elementary agronomy. These programs, which accepted people with no formal education whatever, were significant not simply because of the training they provided but also because of the restructuring of the students' consciousness, taking them beyond immediate practical concerns, expanding their outlook on the world, and bringing them into theoretical spheres of activity.

Secondary schools and technical institutes were then created (a few at first, then more) where young people received more advanced education, beginning with the fundamentals of modern culture and science. The influence of Islam began to disappear; for centuries it had held back the development of independent thought through subjecting people to religious dogma and rigid behavioral standards. All these circumstances created the basis for profound changes in ideology and psychological outlook. Thus the time and place of our research did indeed meet the requirements of our task.

For a work site, we selected remote villages of Uzbekistan and also a few in the mountainous regions of Kirghizia. The ancient high culture of Uzbekistan is still preserved in the magnificent architecture at Samarkand, Bukhara, and Khorezm. Also noteworthy were the outstanding scientific and poetic achievements associated with such figures as Ulug-Bek, a mathematician and astronomer who left behind a remarkable observatory near Samarkand, the philosopher Al-Biruni, the physician Ali-ibn-Sinna (Avicenna), the poets Saadi, Nizami, and others.

As is typical of a feudal society, however, the people remained illiterate and lived in villages, depending completely on the wealthy landowners and powerful feudal lords. The completely unregulated individualistic economy centered on agriculture—mainly cotton growing —and horticulture. Animal husbandry prevailed in the mountainous regions of Kirghizia adjacent to Uzbekistan; cattle-raising families would stay in the mountain pasturelands for many months.

Adherence to the religious leaders' advice was required for any major undertaking. The Islamic religion helped to maintain women's lack of rights. For centuries the women had to remain within the *ichkari* (women's quarters), could leave only if covered by a veil, and would have only a small circle of contacts.

Naturally enough, these regions of the Soviet Union were undergoing especially profound socioeconomic and cultural changes. The period we observed included the beginnings of collectivization and other radical socioeconomic changes as well as the emancipation of women. Because the period studied was one of transition, we were able to make our study to some extent comparative. Thus we could observe both underdeveloped illiterate groups (living in villages) and groups already involved in modern life, experiencing the first influences of the social realignment.

None of the various population groups observed had in effect received any higher education. Even so, they differed markedly in their practical activities, modes of communication, and cultural outlooks. Our subjects comprised the following groups:

1. Ichkari women living in remote villages who were illiterate and not involved in any modern social activities. There were still a considerable number of such women at the time our study was made. Interviews were conducted by women, since they alone had the right to enter the women's quarters.

2. Peasants in remote villages, who continued to maintain an individualistic economy, to remain illiterate, and to involve themselves in no way with socialized labor.

3. Women who attended short-term courses in the teaching of kindergarteners. As a rule, they still had no formal education and almost no literacy training.

4. Active *kolkhoz* (collective farm) workers and young people who had taken short courses. They actively involved themselves in running the farms—as chairmen, holders of kolkhoz offices, or brigade leaders. They had had considerable experience in planning production, in distributing labor, and in taking stock of work output. They dealt with other kolkhoz members and had acquired a much broader outlook than had the isolated peasants. But they had attended school only briefly, and many were still barely literate.

5. Women students admitted to a teachers' school after two or three years of study. Their educational qualifications, however, were still fairly low.

Only the final three groups had experienced the conditions necessary for any radical psychological change. There now existed new motives for action, and also new forms of access to a technological culture and mastery of mechanisms such as literacy and other new forms of knowledge. The transition to a socialist economy brought along new forms of social relations and, with them, new life principles. The first two groups were much less exposed to the conditions for any such fundamental shifts.

We supposed that, for the first two groups, we would find a clear predominance of those forms of cognition that come from immediate graphic-functional* practice, whereas the other subjects would display more mediated thinking. At the same time we expected that the com-

---

*Editor's note: The term "graphic-functional" refers to activity guided by the physical features of objects that the individual works with in practical circumstances.

munication requirements of people doing planned, collectivized farming would have some definite impact on their thinking.

Through a comparison of the mental processes of these groups, we assumed that we could observe the changes caused by cultural and socioeconomic realignment.

## Procedures

Adequate research methods had to include more than simple observation; ours approached a full-fledged experimental inquiry. But such a study inevitably encountered a number of difficulties. A short-term psychological experiment might have proved feasible in the laboratory —where we could have adequately prepared subjects—but highly problematic under field conditions. If newcomers to the villages posed the subjects unusual problems, unrelated to their habitual activities, they might naturally become perplexed or suspicious, since they were unacquainted with us and of course unaware of our motives. The administration of isolated "tests," therefore, could yield data that misrepresented the subjects' actual capabilities. As in any field work with people, then, we emphasized preliminary contact with the population; we tried to establish friendly relations so that the experimental runthroughs seemed natural and unaggressive. Hence we were careful never to conduct hasty or unprepared presentations of the test materials.

As a rule our experimental sessions began with long conversations (sometimes repeated) with the subjects in the relaxed atmosphere of a tea house—where the villagers spent most of their free time—or in camps in the fields and mountain pastures around the evening campfire. These talks were frequently held in groups; even in interviews with one person alone, the experimenter and the other subjects formed a group of two or three, listening attentively and sometimes offering remarks. The talk often took the form of an exchange of opinion between the participants, and a particular problem might be solved simultaneously by two or three subjects, each proposing an answer. Only gradually did the experimenters introduce the prepared tasks, which resembled the "riddles" familiar to the population and thus seemed like a natural extension of the conversation.

Once a problem had been posed, the experimenters went beyond merely recording the answer and always conducted a "clinical" conversation or experiment. A subject's response stimulated further questions or debate; as a result the subject came up with a new answer without interrupting the free-flowing interchange.

To reduce complications in the free discussion (conducted in Uzbek), the experimenter left the actual recording of the results to an assistant who usually placed himself near the discussion group and took care to avoid drawing anyone else's attention. Material was taken down continuously, and only later was a clean copy made and the data processed. This laborious procedure required half a day for a brief session, but it was the only one adequate under the field conditions.

A further requirement for naturalness in the experimental conditions concerned the content of the tasks presented to the subjects. It would have been foolish to give them problems they would have regarded as pointless. Tests developed and validated in other cultures repeatedly produced experimental failures and invalidated our proposed study. Thus we used no standard psychometric tests, and we worked only with specially developed tests that the subjects found meaningful and open to several solutions, each indicating some aspect of cognitive activity. For example, generalization studies could be so contrived that the solution could be either graphic-functional and situational, or abstract and categorical. A subject could solve deductive reasoning problems either by using his available practical experience or by transferring them to a new situation going beyond his experience. The openness of the problems to several solutions permitted a qualitative analysis of the resultant data.

We also introduced some learning tasks in the experiment. By offering to help subjects in certain ways, we tried to show them how, and how much, they could use this assistance in solving a given problem and in proceeding to solve others.

### Research Plan

Our experiments could succeed only if they adequately reflected the major differences in the thinking of people at different stages of sociohistorical development, and could thus reveal a pattern or syndrome. The essential features of mental processes depend on the way they reflect reality; therefore a particular form of mental activity should correspond to a particular level of this reflection.

We hypothesized that people with a primarily graphic-functional reflection of reality would show a different system of mental process from people with a predominantly abstract, verbal, and logical approach to reality. Any changes in the encoding process should invariably show up in the organization of the mental processes behind these activities. In our studies, the subjects could solve the problems either on a concrete, graphic-functional level or on an abstract, verbal, and logical one.

We began with some basic perceptual processes, namely the linguistic encoding of the most salient sensory material. After this introductory stage, we studied the subjects' performance on abstraction and generalization, specifically the comparison, discrimination, and grouping (or classification) of objects—the most fundamental process and a determinant of all the remaining stages.

We assumed that the subjects would be unable to group objects—or even to pick out their abstract features—according to abstract semantic categories. We had every reason to assume that the subjects would recreate graphic-functional situations, and that they would replace dominant abstract meanings with situations involving concrete practical experience. We also had reason to suppose that word meanings would differ markedly (since words are the basic tools of thought), and that experiments in the discovery of word meanings would also reveal large differences in the content of consciousness and in the structure of mental processes. If we reasoned correctly, we could state that our subjects had specific features not only in their systems for encoding perceptual reality, but also in their thought processes themselves. We believed that the system of verbal and logical modes of problem solving and inference would differentiate between our groups of subjects; thinking adequate for practical, graphic-functional experience might serve less well for changing to verbal and logical operations. Therefore we had to study how our subjects perceived logical assumptions and what specific assumptions (graphic-functional or verbal and logical) they used to draw conclusions from them. Our next stage, then, was a psychological analysis of the use of syllogisms whose premises did or did not belong to the system of graphic-functional experience. This stage led to the investigation of reasoning and the psychological analysis of discursive processes, best studied in problem solving. Here we needed to examine how reasoning processes took place, whether they were part of the subjects' direct practical experience, and what changes they underwent when reasoning went beyond graphic-functional practice and into the realm of theoretical or formalized thought. Observation of this type of mental process should uncover some of our subjects' characteristic features of cognitive activity.

The next stage was a study of imaginative processes, the removal of oneself from immediate perception and operation on a purely symbolic, verbal, and logical level. Our material was differences between reproductive and constructive imagination. We assumed that our subjects' capacity for creating abstractions from immediate, graphic-functional experience would be limited and confined to their immediate practice. If we showed this in our subjects, we would obtain another valuable characteristic of practical consciousness whose chief features we were looking for.

The last stage in this sequence was the study of self-analysis and self-consciousness. We hoped to reject the Cartesian notion of the primacy of self-consciousness, with a secondary rank accorded to the perception of the external world and other people. We assumed the reverse: the perception of oneself results from the clear perception of others and the processes of self-perception are shaped through social activity, which presupposes collaboration with others and an analysis of their behavioral patterns. Thus the final aim of our investigation was the study of how self-consciousness is shaped in the course of human social activity.

This plan provided the basic schema for our comparative study and permitted us to achieve our basic aim: a statement of the fundamental psychological shifts that had occurred in human consciousness during a vigorous revolutionary realignment of social history—the rapid uprooting of a class society and a cultural upheaval creating hitherto unimagined perspectives for social development.

# 2

---

## Perception

An analysis of certain features of perception will provide fairly clear evidence about the historical shaping of psychological processes. Traditional psychology treated visual perception as a natural process accessible to investigation by the most elementary natural-science methods. In the study of color perception, for example, early investigators concentrated on physiological processes such as the decomposition of visual purple, color mixture, and color contrast; they assumed that the laws underlying these processes were independent of social practices and remained unchanged over the course of social history. Scientists studying the psychological laws of shape perception also stayed within this natural-science framework. By regarding these phenomena as common to all mankind and unchanging through history, psychologists hoped to find the physiological or even physical laws underlying them.

In the last few decades, however, the development of psychology undermined these naturalistic notions about the relative simplicity and immediacy of perception. The evidence gathered suggests that perception is a complex process involving complex orienting activity, a probabilistic structure, an analysis and synthesis of perceived features, and a decision-making process. In short, perception is a complex process structurally similar to the processes underlying more complex cognitive activities (see Lindsay and Norman, 1972). Examples from color and shape perception demonstrate this claim.

The American psychologist Jerome S. Bruner has correctly noted that every perception is an inherently complex, active process of assigning incoming information to a familiar category, an event intimately involved with the abstraction and generalization functions of language. The human eye can distinguish up to two or three million different hues, but a human being has only twenty or twenty-five color names; a person perceiving a particular hue isolates its primary feature and assigns it to a color category. The same holds true of the perception of geometrical shapes, which rarely match the geometric ideal. Human perception must therefore invariably include the tasks both of isolating the essential features of a shape and of ascribing it to the most similar geometrical category. All computer simulations of perception involve a complex process of analysis and synthesis including "decision making," which assigns any given shape to a particular structural category. Once we recognize that perception is a complex cognitive activity employing auxiliary devices and involving the intimate participation of language, we must radically alter the classical notions of perception as an unmediated process depending only on the relatively simple laws of natural science.

We can thus conclude that, structurally, perception depends on historically established human practices that can alter the system of codes used to process incoming information and can influence the decision assigning the perceived objects to appropriate categories. We can then treat the perceptual process as similar to graphic thinking: it possesses features that change along with historical development.

The historical approach requires us to pay particular attention to the historically established codes involved in the perception even of relatively simple objects and properties. It forces us to doubt whether the laws of color and shape remain forever "unchanging." Indeed, these laws are of a historically limited nature. For example, the familiar forms of "categorical" color perception (red, yellow, green, blue) or shape perception (squares, triangles, trapezoids, and so forth) express only perceptual rules typical of human beings whose consciousness has been shaped under the influence of categories established during some particular time period, notably under the influence of certain concepts learned in school.

How does perception change at different stages in development? What are the relations between perception and practical experience? How can we characterize the perception of people who lack not just schooling but also the conceptual faculties acquired only through systematic instruction? How do subjects designate colors or geometrical shapes, how do they generalize them, and, finally, how do they analyze and synthesize visual forms?

Our hypothesis is that neither the processing of elementary visual information nor the analysis of visual objects conforms to the traditional laws of psychology. Furthermore, we claim that these laws apply only to a relatively brief period of history. Our aim here is to analyze the naming and classification of colors and of geometrical figures. In addition we discuss optical illusions, which also indicate the historical character of visual perception. Our analysis begins with Vygotsky's view that the semantic and systematic nature of psychological processes applies as much to perception as to other mental activities.

The issue of whether color perception changes in accordance with the cultural development of society has been under study for a long time. As far back as the infancy of physiological psychology, investigators observed that the physiological basis of color perception remained unchanged throughout the course of historical development. From the very outset, however, they called attention to the profound structural differences in color vocabularies of different language systems, and also to the possible effects these structures might have on the structure of cognitive processes. Such a hypothesis, first proposed by Humboldt and supported by several linguists, has come to be called the Sapir-Whorf hypothesis: linguistic features have an impact on perception, and on color perception in particular. Languages can distinguish among certain color differences and ignore others, something that inevitably leads to different groupings. Scholars studied color names in the language of the Bible, in African languages (Virchow, 1878, 1879; Rivers, 1901), and differences in color terms in Greek and Indic languages (Allen, 1879; Magnus, 1877, 1880, 1883).

These findings led to several experimental attempts to determine whether differences are restricted to the realm of language or whether they influence, and thus bring about, actual differences in the perception of color. Rivers (1901), for example, performed some experiments with the discrimination and comparison of different colors of wool samples (first used by Holmgren); he concluded that when a language had only one name for blue and green, these colors were often confused. Similar conclusions are found in the work of Woodworth (1905-1906), Ray (1952), Levi-Strauss (1953), Brown and Lenneberg (1954), Lenneberg and Roberts (1956), and Conklin (1955).

These language scientists all note that the absence of special names for groups of colors, or the presence of a large number of subcategories for other colors, is due not to the physiological peculiarities of color perception but to the influence of culture: to the "interest" people have in certain colors and lack of interest in others (Rivers, 1901; Woodworth, 1905-1906; Ray, 1952; Whorf, 1956; and many others). They have also concluded that the wealth of expressions for certain colors and the linguistic poverty of such terms for other colors result from differences in the practical importance that different colors have in different cultures. For example, many languages of people living near the Arctic contain dozens of terms for shades of white (expressions for referring to different types of snow—a fact of practical importance), whereas hues of red and green—of no special importance—are lacking in their vocabulary (see Hunt, 1962; Hoijer, 1954; and others).

In some primitive cultures, categorical color names do not predominate; instead, people use figurative names associating colors with the concrete situations that have practical significance for them (Rivers, 1901, and others). Cross-cultural studies of color-perception nomenclature, therefore, support the conclusions that color names evolve through close association with practice and that they affect perception. How do different forms of practical activity affect color names? What developments in practical activity cause what changes in color names? How does one particular practical activity affect color manipulation, color association, or the comparison, association, and generalization of colors?

PROCEDURE

A subject was presented with a number of colors. He was required to name them and then classify them by dividing them into whatever number of subgroups seemed appropriate in assigning similar colors to a group. Special experiments were run to obtain "forced" groupings. In these trials, subjects had to divide the colors or shapes into a specified number of groups or to evaluate some group put together by the experimenter. To determine the basis for classification, we used objects that resembled each other in some ways but not in others (for example, triangles depicted by solid lines, dotted lines, crosses, and so forth).

There was also a separate experiment involving the evaluation (and classification) of incomplete figures. By seeing how the subjects named and classified incomplete forms, we could check whether the same "laws of perception," which the Gestalt psychologists regarded as invariant in all historical periods, were present in these subjects.

Between fifty and eighty subjects were involved in these experiments; as we have noted, they came from different population groups with varying educational qualifications and experience: ichkari women (illiterate); male peasants (illiterate); collective-farm activists; women students in short preschool courses (barely literate); and women students at a teachers' school. The material was collected by the author, together with L. S. Gazaryants and E. N. Mordkovich.

### Designation and Classification of Color Hues

Most modern languages have a fairly limited array of general names for color categories (yellow, red, blue, green, for example); most of these names have lost any connection they once had with object names, although in a few (orange, raspberry, violet) vestiges of such ties persist. Categorical names are used to denote the overwhelming majority of colors, and object names are used to refer only to a small minority. In modern cultures, moreover, color naming is fairly uniform, but not so in less developed cultures; colors of practical significance are named by a much greater number of terms than are colors of little practical importance.

The assignment of names to colors in Uzbek closely resembles that followed in the other Indo-European languages. One exception is the Uzbek *kok*, which can refer to either green or blue.

*Designation of colors.* Subjects were presented with skeins of wool (or silk) of different hues:

| 1. bright pink | 9. straw-colored | 22. brown |
|---|---|---|
| 2. red | 10-13. shades of green | 23. pale pink |
| 3. claret | 14. black | 24. dark pink |
| 4. dark yellow | 15-17. shades of blue | 25. saturated pink |
| 5. light yellow | 18. sky blue | 26. gray |
| 6. pale yellow | 19. light azure | 27. chestnut |
| 7. lemon yellow | 20. violet | |
| 8. yellow-green | 21. orange | |

The subjects were asked to name these colors. The male collective-farm activists and the female students responded roughly as Moscow schoolchildren and students would. They most often designated colors with categorical names (blue, red, yellow), with occasional refinements (light yellow, dark blue). The subjects sometimes had difficulty naming colors (particularly numbers 16, 18, 19, 23, 24, and 26), and would mention the inadequacy of their vocabulary. Responses frequently ran as follows: "For us Uzbeks, a sewing machine is called a 'machine,' a primus stove a 'machine,' and a tractor also a 'machine.' It's the same with colors. Men don't know colors and call them all 'blue'" (this subject was Yunus., a collective farmer enrolled in an adult course). Object names (pistachio, pomegranate-colored, and so forth) were encountered relatively rarely (16 percent). The ichkari women provided an extreme example of results at the other end of the object-category continuum. They gave richer and more diversified color names than the collective-farm workers and students. The relationship of categorical to graphic object names turned out to be entirely different. The two groups gave about the same number of categorical color names (9 in the first, 7 in the second). The first group, however, gave three times as many modified categorical names. Graphic and object names clearly predominated in the second group (9 in the first, 21 in the second). A short list of graphic and object names encountered in both groups makes the point clear (numbers in parentheses indicate how many times the object name was used).

| Collective farmers and people enrolled in courses | | Ichkari women |
|---|---|---|
| iris (9) | fruit-drop (4) | iris (1) |
| pomegranate (1) | peach (7) | liver (1) |
| peach (2) | pink (1) | spoiled cotton (3) |

| Collective farmers and people enrolled in courses | Ichkari women | |
|---|---|---|
| pistachio (3) | pistachio (10) | brown sugar (1) |
| tobacco (2) | calf's-dung (10) | decayed teeth (1) |
| liver (2) | pig's-dung (10) | cotton in bloom (1) |
| wine (1) | pea (1) | rubbed (1) |
| brick (1) | lake (1) | a lot of water (1) |
| spoiled cotton (7) | sky (1) | hard to translate (3) |
| | poppy (1) | (two versions) |
| | air (1) | |

In terms of distribution frequencies, categorical names predominated in the first group but were relatively infrequent in the second, while the situation was the reverse for graphic and ·figurative names. There was a clear predominance of graphic and object names among ichkari women, and of categorical names among male collective-farm activists.

The summary data for all groups, presented in Table 1, display the same pronounced pattern.

## Color Groupings

Are these differences in color naming reflected in groupings or classifications?

The categorizing of data from the different groups varied. Subjects at a relatively high level of cultural development (collective-farm activists, young people with some short-term formal education) had no difficulty in classifying colors by partitioning them into several groups. They inspected the skeins of wool or silk and divided them up into groups, which they sometimes denoted with the appropriate categorical names and about which they sometimes simply said, "This is the same, but a little lighter" or the like. They usually arranged all the colors into seven or eight groups. When instructed to change the classification and make the groups larger by combining the colors into five groups, they readily did so. Only in a few instances did such subjects begin by grouping the colors according to their saturation or brightness; upon request, however, they readily modified the principle and began to put them into color groups.

Table 1. Figurative Names

| Group | Number of subjects | Figurative names |
|---|---|---|
| Ichkari women | 11 | 59.5% |
| Women in preschool courses | 15 | 30.5 |
| Collective-farm activists | 16 | 16.7 |
| Women at teachers' school | 10 | 16.3 |

The group of ichkari women, however, presented us with an entirely different system. As a rule, the instruction to divide the colors into groups created complete confusion and called forth responses such as, "It can't be done," "None of them are the same, you can't put them together," "They're not at all alike," or "This is like calf's-dung, and this is like a peach." The women usually began by putting different skeins together, then attempted to explain their color groups but shook their heads in perplexity and failed to complete the task. Some subjects replaced the desired grouping by primary color with an arrangement by decreasing brightness or saturation. A resulting series would include pale pink, pale yellow, and pale blue, or a single series of continuous colors with no clear distinctions. Through persistent suggestion, many subjects did solve the problem and break down the colors into groups, but it was obvious that the subjects did so as a concession to the experimenter and that they themselves remained convinced that the colors "were not alike and could not be put together."

About 20 percent of the subjects in this group either continued to refuse to group colors that were "not alike" or broke them down into a large number of small groups. As a rule, this involved a mixed classification, some groups including shades of a certain color (red, green, and the like), others including colors organized by brightness or saturation (dark blue, dark red, and dark green, or light pink, light yellow, and white). These subjects could assign some of the shades of one color to a specific category, that is, give them a unified classification.

The idiosyncratic behavior of the subjects in this group was particularly pronounced in "forced" classification experiments. When told to group the colors into five groups, the subjects refused, claiming that "it can't be done," that then "they would not be alike," or that "dark ones and light ones would be together," or that "they don't go together." It was only when they were asked to use more than five groups that a third of the subjects were able to complete the task; here again, they included shades of different colors, chosen on the basis of brightness and saturation, in each group.

Table 2 shows that a fifth of the ichkari women failed to classify altogether, whereas a fourth replaced the requisite classification by arrangement in continuous series of increasing or decreasing saturation. Only half the subjects were able to break down the hues into isolated groups, these groups including both hues of the same color and hues of different colors of similar brightness and saturation. The other subjects, who grouped the colors according to standard categories, gave no evidence of the same difficulty in classification.

None of the ichkari women broke down the colors into a small number of groups (Table 3). On the contrary, 20 percent of these women showed some tendency to break them down into a number of small groups, combining them according to color, saturation, or brightness. The most typical characteristic of this group was the refusal to make a "forced" classification and a complete inability to

Table 2. Classification of Color Hues (hues grouped according to a mixed principle—color, saturation, brightness)

| Group | Number of subjects | Failure to classify | Arrangement by hues in series | Classification by primary color |
|---|---|---|---|---|
| Ichkari women | 11 | 18.2% | 27.3% | 54.5% |
| Women in preschool courses | 15 | 0 | 6.3 | 93.7 |
| Collective-farm activists | 16 | 0 | 5.8 | 94.2 |
| Women at teachers' school | 10 | 0 | 0 | 100 |

Table 3.  Free and Forced Classification of Color Hues (average number of forms of classification for 25 to 27 hues; percentages)

| Group | Number of subjects | Free classification (number of groups) | | | | | Forced classification | | |
|---|---|---|---|---|---|---|---|---|---|
| | | Refusal | 12-17 | 10-12 | 7-10 | 5-7 | Refusal | 5 | 5 |
| Ichkari women | 10 | 20 | 20 | 10 | 50 | 0 | 70 | 30 | 0 |
| Women in preschool courses | 15 | 0 | 6.1 | 18.3 | 63.4 | 12.2 | 0 | 18.2 | 81.8 |
| Collective-farm activists | 16 | 0 | 5.8 | 35.4 | 58.8 | 0 | 0 | 25 | 75 |
| Women at teachers' school | 10 | 0 | 11.2 | 22.3 | 55.4 | 11.2 | 0 | 57.2 | 42.8 |

partition all the hues into a small number of groups. The other subjects showed not a single instance of failure to make a "forced" classification. Most of the subjects could readily break down the colors into five (or sometimes six or seven) desired categories.

Despite the absence of one-word expressions in Uzbek for denoting standard color categories (similar to those in other languages), the actual use of categorical names and the function they perform in actually classifying colors differed from that in more developed systems.

As we have seen, among ichkari women, who are intimately familiar with embroidery, graphic and object names for colors, rather than categorical ones, are predominant. Accordingly, the process by which they group and classify colors differs markedly from that of assigning them to distinct categories as described in the standard literature on the psychology of color perception and encoding. Well-educated subjects, as a rule, have not only an array of categorical color designations but also put them to use, while our group of subjects employ a quite different classificatory procedure.

A considerable proportion of ichkari women refused to perform any abstract classification operation, replacing it by one of "selecting" colors, and arranging them in a certain spectrum in terms of saturation, brightness, or color combinations. Their color grouping was typically piecemeal. Attempts to obtain a color grouping in which only one primary color would appear in each group—attempts to force them to disengage from their nonmediated color perception—led to failure to perform the task. This unmediated way of relating to colors, without refracting them through the prism of categorical names, is very typical of this first group because their immediate practical experience abounds with such color operations.

This kind of operation with colors disappears in more developed groups where categorical color naming becomes more and more prominent. The latter kind of naming begins to play an important part in the assignment of colors to specific groups. In short, the process of color classification assumes the familiar form of manipulation of color categories abstracted from directly perceived shades of brightness and saturation. We can therefore conclude that profound psychological shifts have taken place.

## THE NAMING AND CLASSIFICATION OF GEOMETRICAL FIGURES

In the first quarter of the twentieth century, one of the most important areas of psychological investigation was the perception of geometrical figures. Gestalt psychologists tried to describe the basic laws of structural perception in order to find the processes that united psychology and physics and that constituted the natural basis of human cognitive processes. An essential feature of their study of geometrical perceptions, however, was that the range of subjects was extremely limited. As a rule, subjects were well educated—usually university-trained, with a thorough academic background in both psychology and geometry. As in the Würzburg school's experiments on the psychology of thinking in which faculty members served as subjects, the work of the Gestalt psychologists on perception of geometrical shapes demonstrated primarily the perception of people with highly specialized training.

Our goal was to determine whether the laws of perception described by the Gestalt psychologists were the same for subjects raised under different socioeconomic systems.

Our hypothesis was as follows. If the perception of geometrical figures involves a process with a complex semantic and system-based structure involving the isolation of key features, a choice from among many alternatives, and an appropriate "decision," this process should depend to a considerable extent on the nature of the practical experience of the subject. A person whose daily activity has been shaped mainly under concrete, graphic-functional, practical conditions will obviously distinguish features and perceive geometrical features differently from one who can draw on theoretical training and a system of well-differentiated geometrical concepts.

Some recent investigators have suggested that the perception of geometrical shapes strongly depends on cultural conditions, and thus differs under different cultural conditions (Hallowell, 1951, 1955; Segall, Campbell, and Herskovits, 1966). Some investigators have observed, for example, that people who live in a "carpentered world" tend to isolate right angles and straight lines while people living under different conditions do not do so (Brunswick and Kamiya, 1953; Segall, Campbell, and Herskovits, 1966). Experiments involving the rotation of a circle about its axis yielded much greater constancy for the Togo people of Africa than for Europeans (Beveridge, 1935, 1939). These scattered observations suggest that the perception of geometrical shapes varies from one culture to another. In particular, these facts suggest that under differing cultural conditions the way people see geometrical shapes, which are real objects, can create patterns of geometrical structural perception differing greatly from those described by the Gestalt psychologists.

Since we wished to check the hunch that shape perception would depend heavily on a subject's practical experience, we conducted a series of tests in which subjects in different groups evaluated or named different geometrical figures and then classified similar ones into separate groups.

To make the analysis (isolation of major features, designation of figures by certain terms, and grouping of figures) to be accessible to investigation, we presented our subjects with geometrical figures belonging to the same category but having different forms. The figures were complete or incomplete, "light" (outlined) or "dark" (solid-colored); they were formed of solid lines or made up of discrete elements (points, crosses, and such; see Fig. 1). We then determined which features the subjects isolated as basic, the categories they assigned particular figures to, and their basis for classifying the figures. As in the preceding series, the subjects were ichkari women, women in preschool courses, kolkhoz activists, and women students at a teachers' school.

**Naming Geometrical Figures**

Only the most culturally advanced group of subjects—the teachers' school students—named geometrical figures by categorical names (circles, triangles, squares, and so forth). These subjects also designated figures made up of discrete elements as circles, triangles, and squares, and incomplete figures as "something like a circle," or "something like a triangle." The subjects gave concrete object names ("ruler," or "meter," for example) only in isolated instances. Subjects in the other group presented us with quite different results.

Ichkari women, as we might expect, assigned no categorical (geo-

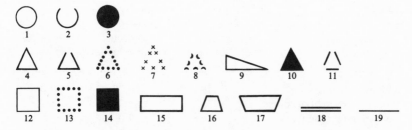

Figure 1. Geometrical figures presented to subjects

metrical) designation to any of the figures presented. They designated all figures with the names of objects. Thus, they would call a circle a plate, sieve, bucket, watch, or moon; a triangle, a *tumar* (an Uzbek amulet); and a square, a mirror, door, house, or apricot drying-board. They treated a triangle made up of crosses as crosswork embroidery, a basket, or stars; they judged a triangle made up of little half-circles to be a gold tumar, fingernails, lettering, and so forth. They never called an incomplete circle a circle but almost always a bracelet or earring, while they perceived an incomplete triangle as a tumar or stirrup. Thus this group's evaluation of abstract geometrical figures was decidedly concrete and object-oriented, and this tendency clearly predominated over abstract geometrical shape perception.

The data obtained from the other groups were intermediate in nature, but all subjects except those attending the teachers' school used predominately specific object-oriented names rather than categorical names (Table 4).

The subjects who perceived shapes in an object-oriented fashion displayed no characteristics corresponding to those described by the Gestalt laws of structural perception. Our subjects interpreted triangles or squares made up of points or crosses as stars, watches, or beads, but generally not as broken representations of triangles or squares. The subjects judged an incomplete circle or triangle as a bracelet, tumar, or device for measuring out kerosene, but not as an incomplete geometrical figure. We have reason to think, therefore, that the laws of "good form" (*prägnanz*) and of structural continuation (or amplification) as described by the Gestalt psychologists are fully apparent only for subjects who have mastered geometrical concepts, and do not appear in people who perceive shapes in an object-

Table 4. Naming of Geometrical Figures (percentages)

| Group | Number of subjects | Object- oriented names | Categorical names |
|---|---|---|---|
| Ichkari women | 18 | 100.00 | 00.0 |
| Women in preschool courses | 35 | 85.3 | 14.7 |
| Collective-farm activists | 24 | 59.0 | 41.0 |
| Women at teachers' school | 12 | 15.2 | 84.8 |

oriented fashion. With careful checking and additional confirmation, this view could play a part in the specific analysis of the psychology of perception of geometrical shapes at different stages of historical development.

**Classification of Geometrical Figures**

In abstract perception, individual geometrical shapes are "representative" of certain major classes (circles, triangles, quadrangles, and so forth); a person whose cognitive processes have been shaped through formal education has no difficulty in assigning these figures to such geometrical classes, even if the figures differ markedly from one another on first impression. The "individual features" of the figures are ignored, the major features of "geometrical class" are isolated, and a "decision" is made on this basis.

What would be the response of subjects whose concrete object-oriented perception of geometrical shapes predominated over abstract geometrical perception and whose process of "encoding" geometrical figures is different? These differences created certain difficulties for figure classification, since the graphic features that functioned as separating factors were intensified, whereas the common features that tended to bring them together were attenuated. For the students in the teachers' school, the classification process differed little from the familiar one: figures were classified into separate categories. As a rule, all types of triangles were combined into one group, and so were all types of quadrangles or circles, regardless of the contour. There were no difficulties whatever in abstracting from the immediate impression created by the external form, color, size, or mode of execution. Categorical names mediated their clearly systematic perception of geometrical figures.

The other subjects presented an entirely different picture. Ichkari women, and to a considerable extent as well male peasants, perceived geometrical figures in an object-oriented way, thus determining their classification. For example, one group of figures included some perceived as the same object; sometimes groups were identified by individual features (color or mode of execution, for example) so that figures similar in either subject content or mode of execution were associated. As a result, the square (12), judged to be a window, and the long rectangle (15), taken to be a ruler, appeared in different groups. Subjects refused to combine them even after appropriate prompting. Conversely, if two figures such as the square and the truncated triangle (12 and 16) were perceived as window-frames ("one is good, the other crooked"), they were readily combined into one group.

The following examples give an idea of how the process of grouping geometrical figures actually took place.

Subject: Alieva, age 26, woman from remote village, illiterate.

19    18    "That's a road, and that's an *aryk* [irrigation ditch]."

5    16    "Window-frame."

6    13    "Watches."

2    3    12    "They're all separate, they aren't alike."

**Could they be arranged differently?**

"These are watches (6 and 13), so they can't be, because how can watches be like anything else? And these window-frames (5 and 16), they can't be put together with the road (19) or the water (18). But this map (12), it could be put with the frames (5 and 16)."

**And could 12 and 18 be put together?**

"No, not at all!"

**Why? Aren't they alike?**

"No, this is a map (12), and this is water in an aryk (18), they don't go together."

**And what about 13 and 12?**

"No, they can't . . . this is a watch (13), and this is a map (12). What would you have if we put them together? How can a map and a watch be put together?"

**Is there really nothing alike in these drawings?**

"The lines are alike; this one (13) is made up of dots, and this one (12) of lines, but the things are different—a watch (13) and a map (12) . . . "

Subject: Shir-Mukham., age 27, woman from remote village, almost illiterate.

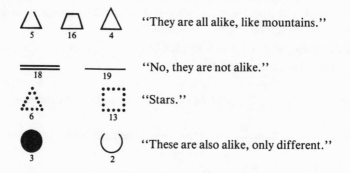

"They are all alike, like mountains."

"No, they are not alike."

"Stars."

"These are also alike, only different."

**Could they be arranged differently so that they would all be alike?**
"No, they couldn't."

**And could these be put together (12 and 15)?**

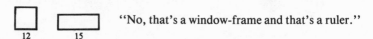

"No, that's a window-frame and that's a ruler."

Subject: Khamid., age 24, woman from remote village.

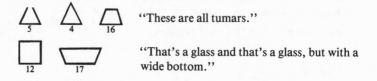

"These are all tumars."

"That's a glass and that's a glass, but with a wide bottom."

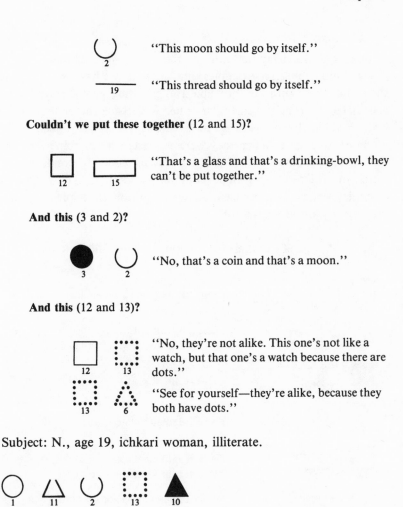

"This moon should go by itself."

"This thread should go by itself."

**Couldn't we put these together** (12 and 15)?

"That's a glass and that's a drinking-bowl, they can't be put together."

**And this** (3 and 2)?

"No, that's a coin and that's a moon."

**And this** (12 and 13)?

"No, they're not alike. This one's not like a watch, but that one's a watch because there are dots."

"See for yourself—they're alike, because they both have dots."

Subject: N., age 19, ichkari woman, illiterate.

The subject defined 1 as a plate, 11 as a tent, 2 as a bracelet, 13 as beads, 10 as a tumar, 4 as a kettle-stand, 16 as a mirror, 5 as a cradle, 8 as a gold tumar, 14 as a mirror, 6 as an Uzbek clock, 7 as a silver tumar, and 12 as a mirror. When asked to classify the figures, she put

7 and 8 together ("they are valuable tumars"), and also 12, 14, and 16 ("mirrors"), declaring that none of the others were similar.

We could proliferate examples, but the facts we have given clearly show that these subjects' principle for grouping geometrical shapes was different from our customary one. A decisive factor here is the way in which the subjects evaluated the figure as an object, or its mode of execution. When they were requested to combine separate figures into groups, they began by seeking concrete conditions in which the figure-objects might commonly "occur." The following examples, which illustrate basic differences in the principle of grouping objects, are of special interest.

Subject: P., age 60, woman from remote village, illiterate.

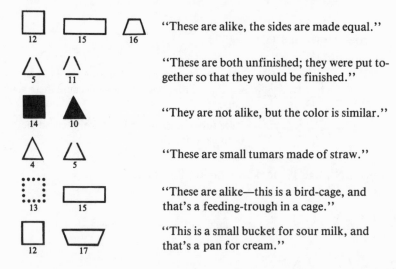

"These are alike, the sides are made equal."

"These are both unfinished; they were put together so that they would be finished."

"They are not alike, but the color is similar."

"These are small tumars made of straw."

"These are alike—this is a bird-cage, and that's a feeding-trough in a cage."

"This is a small bucket for sour milk, and that's a pan for cream."

Subject: Kuis., age 25, woman from remote village, illiterate.

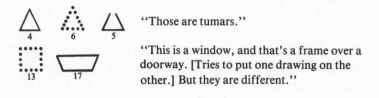

"Those are tumars."

"This is a window, and that's a frame over a doorway. [Tries to put one drawing on the other.] But they are different."

**Could these be put together** (12 and 15)?

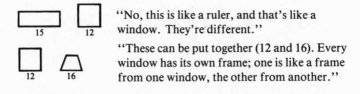

"No, this is like a ruler, and that's like a window. They're different."

"These can be put together (12 and 16). Every window has its own frame; one is like a frame from one window, the other from another."

**And could these be put together** (2 and 3)?

"The shapes are alike, but one is like a watch and the other like a horseshoe, you can put them together but they're not alike."

The examples show the extent to which the perception of subjects who have attended school where they employ abstract geometrical concepts differs from that of subjects who have grown up under the influence only of concrete object-oriented practical activities. The laws of shape perception are the same, but although they dominate the perception of geometrical figures for culturally advanced subjects, they are evaluated as of little importance by the other subjects, who yield to concrete object-oriented perception. Table 5 gives the summary data.

The data show how the principle of classifying geometrical figures varies with changing cultural level, how the percentage of figures grouped on the basis of object-oriented evaluation or direct impression from particular features decreases, and how the percentage of categorical perception increases.

## EXPERIMENTS WITH OPTICAL ILLUSIONS

Optical illusions involve the misperception of certain lines or shapes. The stability and universality of the perceptual illusion have been thought to require some explanation by means of physiological mechanisms common to all people.

The many optical illusions include the familiar Müller-Lyer effect in which two equal lines appear different if oblique cross-pieces attached

Table 5. Classification of Geometrical Figures (percentages)

| Group | Number of subjects | Failure to classify | Classification | | |
|---|---|---|---|---|---|
| | | | object-oriented | in terms of individual graphic features | in terms of geometrical categories |
| Ichkari women | 18 | 21.8 | 20.4 | 57.8 | 0 |
| Women in preschool courses | 35 | 18.3 | 8.4 | 55.0 | 18.3 |
| Collective-farm activists | 24 | 12.8 | 11.6 | 30.8 | 44.8 |
| Women at teachers' school | 10 | 0 | 0 | 0 | 100 |

to their ends are directed inward in one case and outward in the other; the size illusion which "changes" depending whether two identical circles are surrounded by small or large circles; the perspective illusion in which two figures of equal size appear different if they are placed between converging lines that give the impression of perspective; the illusion that arises when one of two equal distances between points is left empty and the other is filled with dots and many others.

The physiological mechanisms underlying these illusions have yet to be adequately studied. Research over the last few decades indicates that illusions depend largely on the motion of one's gaze as it scans the common area occupied by the figure. Most investigators believe that all illusions have a relatively simple physical basis. Rarely has it occurred to them that perceptual illusions might depend on cultural development and appear with different frequencies at different stages of historical development.

According to our hypothesis, all visual perception has a complex semantic and system-based structure that changes with historical development. It incorporates different kinds of visual information processing—sometimes direct impression, at other times refracted through the prism of practical object-oriented experience, and in still others mediated by language and by the forms of analyzing and synthesizing perceived material erected on this basis.

This hypothesis implies another: in the transition to more complex historical conditions of shaping cognitive processes, visual perception also changes.

The changes in mental processes we recorded in observing the perception of geometrical figures should also be manifest with optical illusions. If the mechanisms determining the appearance of illusions are indeed different at different stages of historical development, our research should confirm it. Illusions based on relatively simple physiological factors would probably remain unchanged; those with a more complex basis would manifest themselves differently under different conditions, and perhaps fail to appear at all in certain cases.

For a long time the notion that optical illusions differ in some cultures and that they might result from causes other than elementary physiological laws remained entirely alien to psychologists of perception. As a consequence, the literature on perception contains little data to confirm the view that optical illusions are historically conditioned.

The first investigator to suggest the cultural origins of optical illusions was W. H. R. Rivers (1901), who pointed out that the Toda people of India were much less subject to visual illusions than Europeans. He claimed that there are different classes of illusions, some more closely dependent on cultural conditions than others (for example, the illusion of vertical and horizontal line length was more frequent among the Toda people than the Müller-Lyer illusion).

The cultural and historical conditioning of illusions has received more attention during the past decade. Illusions about geometrical perspective are much more frequent among city-dwellers; among Zulus inhabiting dense forests the trapezoidal-window illusion occurs in only 14 percent of the population, whereas it occurs in 64 percent of the Zulus living in more open environments (Allport and Pettigrew, 1957). Psychologists have advanced the hypothesis that many optical illusions appear only under the economic conditions of city culture (the "carpentered world"), and are encountered much less frequently among forest-dwellers living in circular wattle-and-daub huts. Hence the roots of optical illusions should be sought less in the physiological laws of visual perception than in external social and historical conditions (Segall, Campbell, and Herskovits, 1963, 1966; and others).

In our study (in which Mordkovich and Gazaryants also participated), subjects in different groups observed figures that usually give rise to optical illusions, so as to determine whether these illusions appear in all cases.

We presented various types of illusions (Fig. 2). Some contained differing figure-ground relationships; in others, some distances were "filled in" or not; and still others involved misevaluations of some common area.

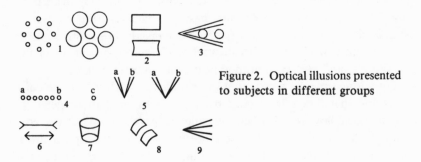

Figure 2. Optical illusions presented to subjects in different groups

We attempted to determine whether the familiar illusion phenomena were present in all our subjects. If optical illusions were not universal, which ones specifically were retained under which conditions, and which ones were not?

It turned out that optical illusions are not universal. The number of illusions fluctuated strongly, increasing to 75.6 percent as the educational level of the subjects rose (Table 6). It became apparent that even among the teachers' school students illusions did not always occur (only in 70-80 percent of the subjects). The number of cases dropped proportionately in groups whose educational qualifications were lower. Thus the data clearly show that *optical illusions are linked to complex psychological processes that vary in accordance with sociohistorical development.*

As Table 6 indicates, the presence of a particular illusion varies from group to group. We can readily distinguish specific geometrical structures that yield a high percentage of illusions among subjects with a higher educational level but that give rise to no such illusions among illiterate subjects.

The Müller-Lyer illusion appears among almost all subjects (see Fig. 2), even among ichkari women (two-thirds of them). Hence, we may assume that the illusion is fairly elementary and independent of cognitive activity. Recent studies (Yarbus, 1965) indicate that eye motion arises from the reflex movement of the eyes over the general area occupied by the figure. This lends a fairly clear explanation to our results.

The illusions perceived primarily by educated subjects include the perspective illusion (3) and others associated with the perception of relationships among geometrical structural elements (5, 7, and 9). There is reason to assume that these illusions result from more complex mental processes and habits acquired through specialized instruction. The perception of perspective, for example, is related to education (Deregowski, 1968a and 1968b).

Our data, however, are preliminary. The mechanisms underlying these illusions might become clearer if we could hit upon a special experiment in which we could vary conditions to produce illusions at will or make them disappear. In our opinion, however, our data clearly show how perceptual processes hitherto regarded as purely

Table 6. Number of Optical Illusions (percentages)

| Group | Number of subjects | Illusion number (see figure 2) | | | | | | | | | Mean |
|---|---|---|---|---|---|---|---|---|---|---|---|
| | | 1 | 2 | 3 | 4 | 5 | 6 | 7 | 8 | 9 | |
| Ichkari women | 9 | 33.3 | 66.6 | 0 | 33.3 | 11.1 | 66.6 | 0 | 11.1 | 33.3 | 29.2 |
| Peasants | 25 | 20.8 | 36.8 | 10.5 | 37.5 | 25.0 | 95.8 | 16.6 | 29.1 | 20.8 | 44.7 |
| Women in preschool courses | 25 | 64.0 | 60.0 | 24.0 | 60.8 | 36.0 | 92.0 | - | - | - | 50.4 |
| Collective-farm activists | 40 | 85.0 | 72.5 | 45.0 | 62.5 | 77.5 | 100.0 | 52.5 | 47.5 | 70.0 | 70.2 |
| Women at teachers' school | 38 | 92.1 | 68.4 | 39.4 | 81.5 | 71.0 | 89.9 | - | - | - | 75.6 |

physiological (and thus universal) are influenced by sociohistorical development.

We began our analysis of how history shapes consciousness by investigating particular psychological processes, specifically forms of perception usually regarded as fairly elementary and suited only to physiological analysis.

The data show that even relatively simple processes involved in perception of colors and geometrical shapes depend to a considerable extent on the subjects' practical experience and their cultural milieu.

The facts thus suggest to us that the conclusions of most current investigations of the perception of color and shape apply in fact only to individuals shaped by cultural and academic influences, that is, persons with a system of conceptual codes for which such perception is adapted. In other sociohistorical conditions in which life experience is basically determined by practical experience and the shaping influence of school has not yet had effect, the encoding process is different because color and shape perception fit into a different system of practical experiences, are denoted by a different system of speech terms and are subject to different laws.

## Research Methods

Subjects were shown drawings of four objects, three of which belonged to one category and the fourth to another. Subjects were asked which three objects were "similar," could be "placed in one group," "designated by one word," as well as which "did not belong in the same group," or could not be designated by the word that applied to the other three.* We used a sample series to demonstrate this mode of classification and provided a detailed explanation of the principles used to include three of the objects (mammals) in one group and to exclude the fourth (a bird). Following this pretraining, we proceeded with the basic observations.

We selected the objects to be classified in such a way that they could be grouped according to one of two principles: (a) reference to a tax-

---

*It should be noted that the Uzbek term *ukhshaidi* has precisely the same meaning as the Russian words for "similar" and "resemble," but that different terms (*moskeldi* or *togrykeldi*) are used to convey the meaning of "appropriate" or "suitable."

onomic category, and (b) participation in a practical situation. A group of objects such as a hammer, a saw, a log, and an ax met these requirements. They could be classified according to the abstract, taxonomic criterion "tools" (hammer, saw, ax) or in keeping with a practical situation ("sawing and chopping wood"). The latter would include those objects used to perform some function in such a situation (saw, log, ax).

These criteria were used to select a number of other object groups such as *glass-saucepan-spectacles-bottle; tree-rose-ear of grain-bird; eye-finger-mouth-ear*. We also used a variant of the test we thought would be most comprehensible to these subjects. In this version we presented drawings of three objects that clearly belonged to one category and asked subjects to select an appropriate fourth object from two or three additional drawings. Generally, only one of the latter fit the first category on the basis of a single semantic criterion. The other (or others) could be grouped with the original three only if the subject used some practical situation as his basis of classification. In this variant of the experiment *ax, chopper, shovel* provided the basic set, and the subject had to choose from *saw, ear of grain, log;* or *tree, flower, ear of grain* formed the basic set to which *rose* or *bird* could be added.

To determine both the reliability of a subject's responses and the specific psychological processes governing them, we asked him to define each group of objects he had compiled. During the course of the discussion we also proposed an alternative solution. Thus, if the subjects had grouped objects according to a practical situation, we told them: "Another fellow solved the problem in a different way." (Put such-and-such objects in one group.) "Why did he do that?" "Was he right or not?" Listening to a subject analyze his own solution as well as that of a hypothetical "other person" revealed more of the psychological processes determining his responses. Hence we were better able to judge how easy it would be for him to shift to another type of classification.

We conducted the experiment in an informal setting—most often in a teahouse where, after a long, leisurely chat with our subjects we would discuss the test material as a kind of "game." Sometimes we administered the experiments simultaneously to two or three subjects, who would study the drawings, discuss them, and frequently interrupt each other to inject their own opinions.

Fifty-five people, ranging in age from eighteen to sixty-five, participated in the experiment. Twenty-six were peasants from the valleys or
mountain villagès of Fergana; some of them farmed the land alone;
others worked in the collective farms that had just been organized; all
of these subjects were illiterate. Ten other subjects were collective-
farm activists who had taken short courses but were barely able to
read and write. Seven young people were students; another twelve,
also young, had attended school for a year or two and were working
on a collective farm.

# 3

## Generalization
## and Abstraction

Experiments on classification have had a long history and now play a
major role in research on cognitive processes. Ach (1905) designed
early tests of object classification in order to describe certain basic
types of logical thinking that would prove that all people had the same
inherent capacity for abstraction and generalization. His tests later
became standard procedure and were used by the eminent psychologists Goldstein (1948) and Vygotsky (1962). Goldstein and his colleague Weigl used them in their pioneering work to distinguish between the object classification of normal and brain-damaged people.
In abstract or categorical classification, the normal subject forms a
distinct category by selecting objects corresponding to an abstract
concept. This kind of classification yields instances of abstract categories such as *vessels, tools, animals,* or *plants* in an appropriate
group, no matter whether the particular objects are ever encountered
together. An ax, saw, shovel, quill, and a knitting needle are all assigned to the category *tools;* a dog, elephant, polar bear, giraffe, and
mouse are similarly assigned to the category *animals.* Both the manner
of object presentation (whether, say, as drawings or toys) and their
size, color, or material are irrelevant. Categorical classification involves complex verbal and logical thinking that exploits language's
capacity for formulating abstractions and generalizations for picking

out attributes, and subsuming objects within a general category. It should be noted that "categorical" thinking is usually quite flexible; subjects readily shift from one attribute to another and construct suitable categories. They classify objects by substance (animals, flowers, tools), materials (wood, metal, glass), size (large, small), and color (light, dark), or other property. The ability to move freely, to shift from one category to another, is one of the chief characteristics of "abstract thinking" or the "categorical behavior" essential to it.

Goldstein and his colleague termed the second type of classification concrete or situational thinking. Subjects who gravitate toward this type of classification do not sort objects into logical categories but incorporate them into graphic-functional situations drawn from life and reproduced from memory. These subjects group together objects such as a table, a tablecloth, a plate, a knife, a fork, bread, meat, and an apple, thereby reconstructing a "meal" situation in which these objects have some use. Clearly, the verbal and logical operation required to abstract certain aspects of objects in order to subsume them under distinct categories of thought do not constitute the psychological basis of this kind of classification. Rather, such an ability hinges on situational thinking, in which objects are grouped not according to some general principle of logic but for various idiosyncratic reasons. Any such group can be extended to include the most diverse objects (all of which, however, apply to a given situation). Moreover, as distinct from categorical systematization, the concrete-situational mode of organization is decidedly rigid. Subjects drawn to it have the greatest difficulty dispensing with visual thought and switching to another principle of classification. Goldstein and his colleagues observed marked instances of this phenomenon in patients with organic brain diseases, particularly among those whose thought processes were not mediated by language.

Vygotsky's work on concept formation coincided with that of Goldstein's, but developed independently with different hypotheses and methods as well as tasks. Goldstein believed that an "abstract orientation" or "categorical thinking" played a major role in determining various methods used to classify perceptual phenomena. Vygotsky interpreted differences in one's reflections of reality as differences in the system of psychological elements that govern such reflections. In his view, language is the most decisive element in systematizing perception; insofar as words are themselves a product of sociohistorical development, they become tools for formulating abstractions and generalizations, and facilitate the transition from unmediated sensory reflection to mediated, rational thinking. He therefore maintained that "categorical thinking" and "abstract orientation" are the consequence of a fundamental reorganization of cognitive activity that occurs under the impact of a new, social factor—a restructuring of the role that language plays in determining psychological activity.

Vygotsky set out to do a more searching analysis of concept formation. He wanted to delineate all the stages in which words figure in one's reflections on reality—to observe how the entire, complex process of concept formation is rooted in the use of words which, he maintained, acquire different meanings at successive stages of development.

In Vygotsky's theory, the idea that the meaning of a word develops —that it signifies different things at different stages, thereby reflecting phenomena in a variety of ways—is based on the assumption that the psychological processes that govern the use of words are themselves subject to change chiefly through socioeconomic factors. Vygotsky quite rightly believed that the study of meaning change would enable psychologists to analyze the semantic and systemic structure of consciousness. He believed that Goldstein's method for studying classification yielded insufficient information, since some subjects had already acquired a fund of experience that already guided them and thus made it impossible to study the formation of new concepts. Vygotsky decided to introduce a method that would allow him to observe how subjects developed completely new concepts. He used much the same method developed by Ach in studying the formation of artificial concepts, the difference being that, in Vygotsky's analysis, the artificial word introduced became the principal agent of concept formation. He thus was able to determine how the word acquired new meaning at the basic stages of development.

Vygotsky observed that a child's procedure for classifying geometrical forms (those which could be designated by one artificial word) varies according to the stage of development. He ascertained the variations that occur in both the logical structure of the concepts a child develops and the psychological processes that enable him to classify phenomena.

During the early stages of a child's development, words are not an organizing factor. Having no logical principle for grouping objects, he perceives each object in isolation and "lumps" them together in a disorderly fashion.

This stage gives way to one that can be considered the first real stage of classification. At this point words still do not figure significantly as an independent means of classification; nonetheless, a child has already begun to compare objects. Such comparison, to be sure, is based strictly on the child's graphic impressions of objects—the physical attributes he singles out. At this stage he can isolate the concrete properties of color, form, or size, and compare two objects on the basis of them. In making these comparisons, however, he quickly loses sight of the attribute he originally singled out, and shifts from one attribute to another. As a result, he assembles a group or chain of objects, each included for various individual reasons. The child has yet to develop a general unified principle of operation; hence, he cannot construct a general unified category. He will group together objects such as a large blue circle (color), a small blue triangle (form), a small green square (size), a small green cube (color), and so on. The group of objects that emerges reflects no unified concept but rather a complex of objects, each included on an individual basis. The logical structure of such a complex, in fact, suggests a family in which one individual is included as a "son," a second a "brother," and a third the "mother" of some central figure. With a more extensive group, one individual may represent the "son" of some central figure, a second—the "wife" of this son, a third—the "wife's brother," and so forth. This type of logical group structure can be detected when objects are incorporated into a general situation in which each participates on an individual basis. (An instance of such grouping is the "meal" situation referred to above: a "chair" would be used to sit at the table; a "tablecloth" to cover it; a "knife" to cut bread.)

The psychological processes governing this way of encoding a characteristic pattern are not based on a word that would allow one to single out a common attribute and denote a category that logically subsumes discrete objects. Rather, the determining factor in classifying objects into complexes is graphic perception or graphic recall of the various interrelations among objects. The intellectual operation fundamental to this classification has not yet acquired the verbal-logical quality of mature thinking but is by nature graphic and memory-based. According to Vygotsky, such thought processes typify older preschool and elementary-school children.

As distinct from this type of thinking, the next stage of development —that of concept formation—is distinctly different. (The transition to this stage is produced by the probably gradual change occurring in a child's whole sphere of activity when he enters school.)

By the time a child reaches adolescence, the logical operations he uses to reflect reality have undergone a marked change, as have the psychological processes that govern his thinking. He no longer generalizes on the basis of his immediate impressions but isolates certain distinct attributes of objects as the basis for categorization; at this point he draws inferences about phenomena by assigning each object to a specific category (by relating it to an abstract concept). He has reached a stage some investigators prefer to designate as the period of "analysis through synthesis." After establishing a sound taxonomic system for subsuming diverse objects under a single category, the adolescent develops a hierarchical conceptual scheme expressing increasingly greater "degrees of community" (for example, rose—flower—plants—organic world). This scheme henceforth determines his whole method for classification. Obviously, once a person has made the transition to this mode of thought, he focuses primarily on the "categorical" relationships between objects, not their concrete mode of interaction.

One can readily understand that the psychological elements governing such taxonomic cognition differ altogether from the processes at work in graphic methods of generalization. The latter are based on an individual's practical experience, whereas at the core of "conceptual" or "categorical" thinking is the shared experience of society conveyed through its linguistic system. This reliance on society-wide criteria transforms graphic thinking processes into a scheme of semantic and logical operations in which words become the principal tool for abstraction and generalization.

There is no question that the transition from situational to taxonomic conceptual thinking is related to a fundamental change in the type of activity one engages in. To the extent that activity is rooted in graphic, practical operations, the latter hinges on the *theoretical* operations a child learns to perform in school.* Since the teacher "programs" this training, it results in the formation of "academic" rather than "mundane" concepts.† Equally important, the transition from visual to conceptual thinking not only affects the role that words assume in a process of codification; it also changes the very nature of words: the meaning they are imbued with. As Vygotsky observed, to the extent that emotional impressions or concrete ideas color the meaning of words in the early stages of development, an historically developed semantic system subsequently governs their meaning, so that words function to produce abstractions and generalizations.

Vygotsky based his theory of the development of meaning and the genesis of new modes of reflection on his observations and research of consecutive stages of child development. It remained for us to clarify the following questions. How does word meaning develop with consecutive stages of human society? Does a well-educated person's capacity for generalization hold true of adults in all societies? Do sociohistorical systems with diverse cultural patterns develop modes of generalization that reflect reality in distinctly different ways? Is the procedure for categorizing objects according to essential properties characteristic of adult thinking everywhere? Or do more concrete methods of generalization prevail in societies where rudimentary types of activity predominate? If in fact different social systems produce different kinds of generalization, what effect will cultural and historical advances have on a person's pattern of thinking? Will he retain his habitual approach to generalization or will his exposure to new types of activity, particularly those inculcated in education, produce a radical change in the method he prefers? Given the profound transformations a social order undergoes when the mass of its population becomes literate, what changes occur in their cognitive processes?

## RESULTS
As noted earlier, the majority of our subjects had never attended school and hence had no systematic training in theoretical operations.

---

*It should be noted that studies of child development have yet to clarify the precise nature of such practical activity.

†In his classic work *Language and Thought* (1962), Vygotsky provided a detailed account of the distinction between these two types of concepts.

Consequently, we were all the more curious to observe what principles they would apply in grouping objects.

Almost all the subjects listened to the instructions attentively and set to work eagerly. Yet often—even from the outset—instead of trying to select "similar" (*ukhshaidi*) objects, they proceeded to select "objects suitable for a specific purpose." In other words, they replaced a theoretical task by a practical one: to reproduce the practical relationships among objects. This tendency became apparent early in the experimental session when subjects immediately began to evaluate objects in isolation and designate their functions ("this one" is needed for such-and-such a job, "that one" for another). They saw no need to compare and group objects in abstract terms and assign them to specific categories.* Later on in the experiment many of the subjects were able to overcome this tendency. Even then, however, they tended to deal with the task as one of grouping objects according to their role in a practical situation and not as a theoretical operation of categorizing them according to some common attribute. In other words, they reproduced procedures drawn from their daily work experience. As a result, they grouped objects strictly on an idiosyncratic basis, reconstructing a graphic situation in which the objects could function together.

Moreover, these subjects did not interpret words as symbols of abstract categories usable for classifying objects. What mattered to them were strictly concrete ideas about practical schemes in which appropriate objects could be incorporated. Consequently, their thinking was wholly unlike that of subjects trained to perform theoretical operations.

Our subjects used concrete, "situational" thinking to compile groups that were extremely resistant to change. When we tried to suggest another group (based on abstract principles), they generally rejected it, insisting that such an arrangement did not reflect the intrinsic relationships among the objects, that a person who adopted it was "stupid," "did not understand anything." Only in rare instances did they concede the possibility of employing such means of classification, doing so reluctantly, convinced it was not "important." Only classifi-

*Editor's note: Here and throughout this chapter Luria uses the terms "abstract" or "logical" classification to refer to classification that selects items belonging to the same taxonomic category.

cations based on practical schemas struck them as "important," or "right."

The tendency to reproduce operations used in practical life was *the* controlling factor among uneducated, illiterate subjects. By contrast, subjects whose activities were still confined primarily to practical work but who had taken some courses or attended school for a short time were inclined to use both modes of generalization, practical and theoretical (though the former clearly predominated).

A third group of subjects, primarily young kolkhoz activists with only a year or two of schooling, not only grasped the principle of categorical classification but employed it as their chief method of grouping objects. They found it comparatively easy to shift from situational to abstract thinking; for them, even a brief period of training had produced results.

Consequently, we have every reason to conclude that although our subjects preferred to group objects according to practical schemas— considering these more fundamental and appropriate to their daily lives—they had some capacity for engaging in complex, abstract cognitive activities. To illustrate these generalizations, we quote a number of experimental protocols.

Subject: Rakmat., age thirty-nine, illiterate peasant from an outlying district; has seldom been in Fergana, never in any other city. He was shown drawings of the following: *hammer-saw-log-hatchet.*

> "They're all alike. I think all of them have to be here. See, if you're going to saw, you need a saw, and if you have to split something you need a hatchet. So they're *all* needed here."
>
> *Employs the principle of "necessity" to group objects in a practical situation.*

We tried to explain the task by another, simpler example.

> **Look, here you have three adults and one child. Now clearly the child doesn't belong in this group.**
>
> "Oh, but the boy must stay with the others! All three of them are working, you see, and if they have to keep running out to fetch things, they'll never get the job done, but the boy can do the running for them . . . The boy will learn; that'll be better, then they'll all be able to work well together."
>
> *Applies same principle of grouping.*

Look, here you have three wheels and a pair of pliers. Surely, the pliers and the wheels aren't alike in any way, are they?

"No, they all fit together. I know the pliers don't look like the wheels, but you'll need them if you have to tighten something in the wheels."

*Again assigns objects functions in a practical situation.*

But you can use one word for the wheels that you can't for the pliers— Isn't that so?

"Yes, I know that, but you've got to have the pliers. You can lift iron with them and it's heavy, you know."

Still, isn't it true that you can't use the same word for both the wheels and the pliers?

"Of course you can't."

We pick up with the original group: *hammer-saw-log-hatchet.*

Which of these things could you call by one word?

"How's that? If you call all three of them a 'hammer,' that won't be right either."

*Rejects use of general term.*

But one fellow picked three things—the hammer, saw, and hatchet— and said they were alike.

"A saw, a hammer, and a hatchet all have to work together. But the log has to be here too!"

*Reverts to situational thinking.*

Why do you think he picked these three things and not the log?

"Probably he's got a lot of firewood, but if we'll be left without firewood, we won't be able to do anything."

*Explains selection in strictly practical terms.*

True, but a hammer, a saw, and a hatchet are all tools.

"Yes, but even if we have tools, we still need wood—otherwise, we can't build anything."

*Persists in situational thinking despite disclosure of categorical term.*

Subject is then shown drawings of: *bird-rifle-dagger-bullet.*

"The swallow doesn't fit here . . . No . . . this is a rifle. It's loaded with a bullet and kills the swallow. Then you have to cut the bird up with the dagger, since there's no other way to do it."

*Rejects attempts at categorical classification; reverts to situational thinking to include all objects.*

"What I said about the swallow before is wrong! All these things go together!"

**But these are weapons. What about the swallow?**

"No, it's not a weapon."

**So that means these three go together and the swallow doesn't?**

"No, the bird has to be there too, otherwise, there'll be nothing to shoot."

Is shown drawings of: *glass-saucepan-spectacles-bottle.*

"These three go together, but why you've put the spectacles here, I don't know. Then again, they also fit in. If a person doesn't see too good, he has to put them on to eat dinner."

**But one fellow told me one of these things didn't belong in this group.**

"Probably that kind of thinking runs in his blood. But I say they all belong here. You can't cook in the glass, you have to fill it. For cooking, you need the saucepan, and to see better, you need the spectacles. We need all four of these things, that's why they were put here."

*Replaces initial attempt to group together "cooking vessels" with search for practical scheme in which objects are interrelated.*

Subject: Mirzanb, age thirty-three, uneducated; works in a village; has been in Fergana once, never in any other city. Is shown drawings of: *glass-saucepan-spectacles-bottle.*

"I don't know which of the things doesn't fit here. Maybe it's the bottle? You can drink tea out of the glass—that's useful. The spectacles are also useful. But there's vodka in the bottle—that's bad."

*Uses principle of "utility" to classify objects.*

**Could you say that the spectacles don't belong in this group?**

"No, spectacles are also a useful thing."

Subject is given a complete explanation of how three of the objects refer to the category of "cooking vessels."

**So wouldn't it be right to say the spectacles don't fit in this group?**

"No, I think the bottle doesn't belong here. It's harmful!"

**But you can use one word—vessels—for these three, right?**

"I think there's vodka in the bottle, that's why I didn't take it . . . Still, if you want me to . . . But, you know, the fourth thing [spectacles] is also useful."

*Disregards generic term.*

"If you're cooking something you have to see what you're doing, and if a person's eyes are bothering him, he's got to wear a pair of glasses."

**But you can't call spectacles a vessel, can you?**

"If you're cooking something on the fire, you've got to use the eye-glasses or you just won't be able to cook."

Subject: Sher., age sixty, illiterate peasant from the village of Yardan. The task is explained through the example, *shirt-boots-skullcap-mouse,* and subject shown pictures of the following: *hammer-saw-log-hatchet.*

"They all fit here! The saw has to saw the log, the hammer has to hammer it, and the hatchet has to chop it. And if you want to chop the log up really good, you need the hammer. You can't take any of these things away. There isn't any you don't need!"

*Replaces abstract classification with situational thinking.*

**But in the first example I showed you that the mouse didn't fit in.**

"The mouse didn't fit in! But here all the things are very much alike [*ukhshaidi*]. The saw saws the log, and the hatchet chops it, you just have to hit harder with the hammer."

**But one fellow told me the log didn't belong here.**

"Why'd he say that? If we say the log isn't like the other things and put it off to one side, we'd be making a mistake. All these things are needed for the log."

*Considers idea of utility more important than similarity.*

**But that other fellow said that the saw, hammer, and hatchet are all alike in some way, while the log isn't.**

"So what if they're not alike? They all work together and chop the log. Here everything works right, here everything's just fine."

**Look, you can use one word—tools—for these three but not for the log.**

"What sense does it make to use one word for them all if they're not going to work together?"

*Rejects use of generalizing term.*

**What word could you use for these things?**

"The words people use: saw, hammer, hatchet. You can't use one word for them all!"

**Could you call them tools?**

"Yes, you could, except a log isn't a tool. Still, the way we look at it, the log has to be here. Otherwise, what good are the others?"

*Employs predominantly situational thinking again.*

The examples cited indicate that we had no luck getting these subjects to perform the abstract act of classification. Even when they grasped some similarity among various objects, they attached no particular importance to the fact. As a rule, they operated on the basis of "practical utility," grouping objects in practical schemes rather than categorizing them. When we referred to a generic term they could use to designate a distinct group of objects, they generally disregarded the information or considered it immaterial. Instead, they adhered to the idea that objects should be grouped in practical arrangements. They continued to do so even when we presented objects that, in our view, would be difficult to group together for some genuinely practical scheme. When we clarified the principle of abstract classification, they listened attentively enough to our explanation but failed to take it into account. The following examples illustrate this tendency.

Subject: Abdy-Gap., age sixty-two, illiterate peasant from remote village. After the task is explained, he is given the series: *knife-saw-wheel-hammer.*

"They're all needed here. Every one of these things. The saw to chop firewood, the others for other jobs."

*Evaluates objects in terms of "necessity" instead of classifying them.*

**No, three of these things belong in one group. You can use one word for them that you can't for the other one.**

"Maybe it's the hammer? But it's also needed. You can drive nails in with it."

The principle of classification is explained: three of the objects are "tools."

"But you can sharpen things with a wheel. If it's a wheel from an *araba* [kind of bullock cart], why'd they put it here?"

Subject's ability to learn the principle of classification is tested through another series: *bayonet-rifle-sword-knife.*

> "There's nothing you can leave out here! The bayonet is part of the gun. A man's got to wear the dagger on his left side and the rifle on the other."

> *Again employs idea of necessity to group objects.*

> The principle of classification is explained: three of the objects can be used to cut but the rifle cannot.

> "It'll shoot from a distance, but up close it can also cut."

> He is then given the series *finger-mouth-ear-eye* and told that three objects are found on the head, the fourth on the body.

> "You say the finger isn't needed here. But if a fellow is missing an ear, he can't hear. All these are needed, they all fit in. If a man's missing a finger, he can't do a thing, not even move a bed."

> *Applies same principle as in preceding response.*

> Principle is explained once again.

> "No, that's not true, you can't do it that way. You have to keep all these things together."

One could scarcely find a more clear-cut example to prove that for some people abstract classification is a wholly alien procedure. Even when we explained the principle of classification very thoroughly, the subjects persisted in their own approach.

The features characteristic of that approach were demonstrably apparent in group experiments, where the issue of how objects should be grouped provoked lively discussion. The following are just two examples of the responses such experiments elicited.

The participants included: Kar. Farf., age twenty-five (I); Yarb Mamar., age thirty-two (II); Mad. Suleim, age twenty-six (III). All three subjects, illiterate peasants from the village of Palman, had either never been in a city or visited one only on rare occasions. The following series was presented: *hammer-saw-log-hatchet.*

> I.    "They're all alike. The saw will saw the log and the hatchet will chop it into small pieces. If one of these things has to go, I'd throw out the hatchet. It doesn't do as good a job as a saw."

> *Includes objects in practical situation.*

II.  "I also think they're all alike. You can saw the log with the saw, chop it with the hatchet, and if it doesn't split, you can beat on the hatchet with the hammer."

The task is clarified through another example: three caps and a shirt.

II.  "No, you can't take any of these out. All four of them are alike. You can wear the skullcap and also the shirt. All that's missing here are some boots and one other thing—a belt."

I.  "Yes, these four are alike."

III.  "I'd throw out the skullcap, it's old-fashioned and doesn't look good with the shirt."

Once again the principle is explained; the caps are worn on the head, the shirt on the body.

I.  "No, that's not right. Anyway, I'd get rid of the skullcap, it's old-fashioned."

**But is the shirt something you can put on your head?**

I.  "If there was a really nice shirt next to it, and a pair of trousers and some boots, I'd wear one of the caps to work and put the other on when I went to the teahouse."

*Persists in concrete thinking despite explanation of principle used in abstract classification.*

**Wouldn't it be right to say that the caps are things you wear on your head, whereas the shirt isn't?**

"Yes, you could put it that way. Yes, of course."

**So the fellow who took the shirt out of this group was right?**

"Yes, a little bit."

*Acknowledges possibility of both methods but considers abstract classification only partially correct.*

We go back to the original series: *hammer-saw-log-hatchet.*

I.  "It's the hammer that doesn't fit! You can always work with a saw, but a hammer doesn't always suit the job, there's only a little you can do with it."

II.  "You can throw out the hammer, because when you saw a log, you have to drive a wedge into it."

Same tendency as before.

**Yet one fellow threw out the log. He said the hammer, saw, and hatchet were all alike in some way, but the log is different.**

III.  "If he wants to make planks, he won't need the log."

I.   "If we're getting firewood for the stove, we could get rid of the hammer, but if it's planks we're fixing, we can do without the hatchet."

*Grouping varies with situation depicted.*

**If you had to put these in some kind of order, could you take the log out of the group?**

I.   "No, if you get rid of the log, what good would the others be?"

**But these three things are tools—right?**

I.   "Yes, they're tools."

**What about the log?**

All three subjects: "It belongs here too. You can make all sorts of things out of it—handles, doors, even the handles of tools are made out of wood!"

II.   "We say it's a tool because everything's made out of wood, so it belongs with the others."

**Supposing I put a dog here instead of the log?**

I.   "Then the dog wouldn't fit, it goes with the rifle." [Points to next series of drawings.]

*Creates new situation.*

**Then these three things would be alike in some way?**

II.   "If it was a mad dog, you could beat it with the hatchet and the hammer and it would die."

*Persists in predominant approach: objects grouped strictly according to practical uses.*

**Still, aren't these three things alike in some way?**

II.   "No, what's missing here is a man, a worker. Without him, there's nothing alike about these things."

III.   "You've got to have the wood here! There's nothing alike about these things unless the log's here. If you keep the log, they're all needed, but if you don't, what good are they?"

**Yet you can use one word—tools—for these, isn't that so?**

All three subjects: "Yes, of course."

**And you can't use that word for a log?**

"No."

**That means these three have some likeness?**

"Yes."

**If I asked you to pick the three things you could call by one word, which would you pick?**

I. "I don't understand."

II. "All four of them."

III. "If we don't pick the log, we won't have any need of the other three."

*Substitutes arguments about practical functions for use of generic term.*

**But one fellow told me that a log isn't a tool. After all, it can't chop, it can't saw.**

III. "No, whoever told you that must have been crazy. To make a tool you need a log. Part of the log goes into making the handle of a saw, so the power of a log also goes into cutting. The log can't cut by itself but together with the hatchet it can."

**But I couldn't call a piece of wood a tool, could I?**

III. "Yes you could. Handles are made out of it."

II. "Take this mulberry tree—you can make handles of tools out of it."

After a lengthy discussion of the objects one can call "tools," we gave subjects the following series: *glass-saucepan-spectacles-bottle.*

III. "The saucepan and the spectacles fit together. The glass goes very well with the bottle. If it's full of vodka, you can go off to a shady spot and have yourself a good drink. Nice! Those really go together!"

*Considers objects that "fit together" those that are needed in a concrete situation.*

III. "We can eat noodles out of the saucepan, but we don't need the spectacles."

**But we have to pick three things that are alike in some way.**

II. "The bottle doesn't fit here. It's got liquor in it and that costs a lot of money."

*Applies same principle.*

III. "Let me tell you that if I had a lot of money, I'd buy the bottle and drink the vodka."

**If you had to choose three things according to a common feature, what would that be?**

II. "If I picked the glass, it's because I'd need it for drinking tea. The saucepan's good for cooking, and the spectacles for a person whose eyes bother him. Even if you have a pain only once a year, the spectacles still come in handy. Look, you know, all these things are sold in the shops because people need them. So you have to pick all of them."

**But one fellow took the spectacles away, said they were a different kind of thing.**

II. "No! He's a fool! What's a person supposed to do if his eyes hurt?"

**But the other three are cooking vessels (idish), isn't that so?**

II. "In its way the other one's a vessel too."

**But these things all have to do with food.**

III. "Yes, but when a fellow gets to be thirty or forty years old, don't you think he needs spectacles?"

**Sure, but you're supposed to pick three things that are alike in some way, and the spectacles are different.**

II. "When you get right down to it, none of the things are alike. Sure, the bottle's like the glass, and the saucepan's like our boiling pans. And the spectacles are for your eyes."

*Groups according to practical interaction of objects, not similar attributes.*

**Could you put the bottle and the spectacles and the glass together in one group? How are they alike?**

III. "You can put the bottle and the glass together, but not the spectacles—they'll get rusty. You've got to wrap them up in some paper."

*Construes "put together" in a logical order to mean "place side by side."*

**Still, couldn't you say that they're all made of the same material?**

All three subjects: "Yes, they're all made of glass."

**So it means they can go in one group?**

II. "Yes."

III. "No, the spectacles could get rusty, they've got to be set aside."

II. "But the bottle and the glass are very much alike; when the bottle gets dirty, you can rinse it out with the glass."

*Objects grouped in practical situation, not classified.*

One can see that we failed to get these subjects to shift to a logical plane of thought. The fact that objects had "similar" attributes seemed to them irrelevant; consequently, they repeatedly introduced a concrete situation in which the objects could function together.

We obtained similar results with another variant of the tests. In this "selective" version, we showed subjects drawings of two or three objects, then presented a supplementary group of two or three others from which they were to pick one that related to the first group, one "similar" to it. As a rule, subjects disregarded objects that pertained to the same abstract category as the original group and selected those that could function together in some practical fashion. The following typify the results obtained in this version of the experiment.

Subject: Shir., age fifty-seven, illiterate peasant from village of Yardan. He was shown illustrations of *ax-sickle* and asked to select a similar type of object from a second group consisting of *saw-log-ear of grain*.

**Which one of these is most like the kind of things in the other group?**

"If you want them to be the same, you'd have to pick the ear of wheat. A sickle reaps grain, so this ear will be plucked by this sickle."

*Selects objects in terms of practical functions.*

**Will the three things really be the same type then?**

"No, the ax isn't as much like the wheat as the sickle. The ax should go with the log—it can chop it."

**But you have to pick one thing so that you'll have three which are all alike, the same type.**

"Then it has to be the ear of wheat. That'll leave the saw and the log over there—those two are alike."

*Replaces abstract idea of "similarity" with practical notion of "suitability."*

**Are those things really alike?**

"No, you have to set them up this way. Move the ear of wheat closer to the sickle so that it will cut it, and put the ax in the log so they'll be together."

**Then they'll really be like one another?**

"Yes, very much alike."

**Supposing the ax wasn't close to the log?**

"Then they wouldn't be alike. But if you put them next to each other, the ax can chop the log. They'll be very much alike then and very handy. See, we hire a worker by the day to chop firewood. Now, if the ax is going to be set somewhere far off from the log, he'll have to waste a lot of time hunting for it."

*Uses practical situation rather than classification to determine relationship between objects.*

**No, let me explain. Is an ax like a sickle in some way—is it the same type of thing?**

"Yes, they're both tools."

**What if I were to put some barley here?**

"No, that wouldn't be right. Barley is food, it's not an asbob."

*Spontaneous use of categorical term.*

**Would the group be alike if I put the barley here?**

"It would because you can chop with the ax, reap with the sickle, and eat the barley."

**Supposing I put the saw here?**

"Yes, that would fit. A saw is also a tool."

*Reinforcement of the principle of categorical classification.*

After using a number of simple examples to explain the principle of classification once again, we reminded the subject that he was to apply this rule in grouping the next series of objects. Then we tested his ability to do so by giving him the objects *tree-ear of grain* and a group of alternatives consisting of: *bird-rosebush-house.*

"Naturally, you've got to pick the rosebush."

**Why?**

"This is a tree, this is a flower [ear of grain], this is a bird, this is a rosebush. You could also let the bush stay where it is, then it'll grow next to the house."

*Groups objects in an imaginary situation.*

**But if you had to form a group of the same type, which thing would you pick?** [By way of example, we reminded him of the principle used to group "tools" together.]

"Then I'll have to pick the rosebush. They'll all be trees then. But the bird will stay there underneath. It will keep an eye on the trees—it loves growing things."

*Adopts abstract classification but immediately reverts to situational thinking.*

Subject is given another series: *horse-ram* along with the supplementary group (*camel-bucket-house*). The instructions are repeated and subject reminded of the principle used to group "tools" together.

**Which should you pick to get one kind of group?**

"The camel has to go over here—then they'll all be animals. It'll be very good to have them all stand together."

*Begins classifying according to abstract principle but immediately lapses into visual thinking.*

**That means the bucket and the house don't fit with the others?**

"It's right to let them stay where they are. The bucket should be next to the house—a bucket is a very useful thing. You see, the horse, sheep, and camel have to stay here, since they're all living things. But the things down here also fit in. A family can use them all."

*Indicates that in his mind the two principles of grouping coexist.*

The examples illustrate that even when a subject appeared to have learned the principle of abstract classification, his grasp remained far from firm. As he proceeded to think through a problem, he would revert to his habit of constructing imaginary situations in which objects functioned together. Here, as in the preceding tests, his thought was primarily practical. A large number of tests corroborated this fact. We need cite only a few of the resultant responses from a second group experiment.

Participants: Yarb. Madmar, age thirty-two (I), and Madaz. Suleim., age twenty-six (II), illiterate peasants from Palman. After a detailed explanation of the task, they were given the objects *ax-sickle-hatchet* and asked to complete the series by selecting one of the following: *saw-ear of grain-log.*

I.   "You have to put the ear of wheat here."

II.  "Then you'll have to take the ax out and put it next to the log."

*Once again objects are grouped according to their practical interrelationships.*

**No, you can't take anything out of the first group. You have to add one from the other group, so that you'll have four things you can call by one word.**

I.   "Then you should put the ear of wheat there."

**What if I were to put the saw here?**

I.   "Then you could call them tools. The ear of wheat fits in too, but in a different way."

*Perceives two possible schemes of grouping.*

In order to determine whether subjects had grasped the principle, we gave them another series: *tree-ear of grain (rosebush-bird-house).*

II.  "The swallow has to go here, only you shouldn't put it next to the tree but on a branch so it will sing."

**No, you're supposed to add one thing so that you'll have a group you can call by one word.**

I.  "Then it's got to be the flower. They'll all be like the tree then."

II.  "But the bird also flies over to the tree, it doesn't just sit in one place all the time."

*Masters the principle of classification, but reverts to situational thinking again.*

There is no point quoting additional responses since their marked uniformity merely confirms our conclusions about these subjects' manner of thinking. Objects pertaining to a distinct category were grouped either according to the practical principle of necessity or interrelated in a graphic situation. Our repeated references to generic terms (tools, vessels, animals) were of some help to these people in classifying objects categorically. Yet they regarded such abstract principles of classification as inconsequential and quickly reverted to the tendency to reconstruct situations in which the objects could function as a group.

Such graphic, situational thinking was *the* controlling factor with illiterate peasants from remote areas who farmed the land alone and had never spent any time in a large city. On the other hand, our second group of subjects—people who either had taken short courses or had become involved in the communal work of the newly organized collective farms—had reached a certain transitional stage. They were able to employ categorical classification as an alternative to practical grouping. This is apparent from the following examples.

Subjects: Kurb., age fifty, illiterate collective-farm worker (I); Khaidar, age twenty-six, barely literate, has spent considerable time among Russians (II). Series presented: *hammer-saw-log-hatchet.*

II. "The hammer doesn't belong here. The hatchet chops the log, the saw saws it, but the hammer doesn't fit in. Then again, if you saw the log, you'll have to drive a wedge in, so you'll need the hammer."

*Begins by using situational thinking.*

I. "No, you don't need the hammer here, you can use the hatchet."

**But can you say that a saw, hatchet, and a log are the same types of things?**

II. "Sure they're alike, they work together."

I. "You can chop down a tree with a *ketmen* [tool resembling a mattock] but you first have to dig up the roots. So, these two things are alike."

*Interprets "similar" to mean "effect produced by interaction of objects."*

**In what way is a saw like a log?**

I. "They're needed together because they work to chop down a tree. They're alike in the work they do. If you take the hatchet away, you won't be able to do anything with the log, and you can't saw unless you've got a saw."

*Same tendency apparent in this response.*

**I understand that you use a saw and a hatchet on one job, but are logs and hatchets the same type of things?**

I. "They don't look alike, but they're alike in the work they do."

II. "No, they're not. The saw is a metal tool whereas the log is made of wood."

*Singles out attribute as a basis of categorization.*

**So which things should you group together?**

II. "The log is different. The others are all metal tools. But since you drew them all together we thought the log belonged here too."

*Solves task; categorizes objects.*

**Name some other tools.**

II. "Ax, plane, saw, hammer, sickle."

**So we've sorted out the things that are alike here. Can you say that a hatchet is like a log?**

II. "No, you can't."

I. "That's not true. I need the saw to saw the log and the hatchet to split it!"

II. "You don't understand—these are tools!"

I. "No, you have to use the saw on the log, and if you take the log away there'll be nothing for the saw to do."

*Responses indicate a conflict between two levels of classification: theoretical (conceptual) and practical (situational).*

After principle of classification is explained again, subjects are given an additional series: *glass-saucepan-spectacles-bottle.*

I. "The saucepan and the glass are alike—you can pour from the saucepan into the glass. And the spectacles are like the bottle because most likely it has ink in it."

*Groups objects in graphic-functional situation.*

**Which three are alike in some way?**

I. "Must be the saucepan, glass, and bottle because you can pour from one into the other. But while a person's doing that he has to put on the spectacles."

*Establishes similarity of objects' functions.*

**Which one of the things doesn't belong here?**

I. "Doesn't the bottle fit here?"

**You're supposed to find three things that are alike. Which three can you call by one word?**

I. "The bottle, the spectacles, and the glass are the same. The glass, the spectacles, and the bottle were probably all made in one factory. They're all glass!"

*Solves task.*

**One fellow told me the saucepan, bottle, and glass are alike in some way. Why did he say that?**

I. "No, that's not right. These are all made of glass. The only difference is that you can pour into the others and you can't do that with the spectacles. But the point is they're all made of glass."

These responses clearly indicate the conflict that can exist between the two types of classification. The younger subject easily learned how to assign objects to an abstract category. On the other hand, the older man had to struggle between a tendency to employ both methods—graphic and abstract—though eventually he learned to apply the latter. The same results were obtained from the second group of subjects in another variant of the test, the "selective" version referred to previously.

Subject: Khalil, age forty-nine, illiterate peasant. Was given the series *ax-sickle-hatchet* and asked to pick a similar object from a supplementary group (*saw-ear of grain-log*).

"The saw belongs here. If you've got an ax you definitely need a saw. A saw also goes well with a hatchet, but for the sickle you need an ear of wheat."

*Groups objects in terms of practical, situational thinking.*

**You have to pick only one thing that will fit in with the first three.**

"My first choice is the saw, then the ear of wheat."

**Which would be more correct?**

"If I've got to pick only one, it'll have to be the saw. But then I'd have to take out the sickle and put in the log. You need a sickle for an ear of grain and a saw to saw a log. Then you have to split it with an ax."

*Persists in use of situational thinking.*

**But the whole first group has to be alike, the same kinds of things.**

"Then I'll take the ear of wheat, because we need wheat most of all."

*Employs attribute of "necessity."*

**But could you pick the ax, sickle, and saw?**

"No, the ear of wheat has to be near the sickle and the saw has to be next to the ax."

*Uses practical situation again.*

**But all these are farming tools.**

"Sure, but each one's connected with its own job."

*Acknowledges possibility of categorical classification but considers it immaterial.*

Subject is then given the series *tree-ear of grain* to match with one of the following (*bird-rosebush-house*).

"There should be a house next to the tree and the flower [ear of grain]."

*Uses practical scheme of grouping.*

**But is a house really like a tree in any way?**

"If you put the rosebush here, it won't be of any use to a person, but if you put the house here, a person could live in it and have beautiful things around him. The rosebush can't go in the shade, because we want it to bloom."

*Again employs idea of utility and groups in practical terms.*

**But are trees and a house alike in any way?**

"They don't look alike but they go very well together. If you want to pick the one that's alike, you've got to pick the rosebush."

*Shifts to categorical classification after attention is focused on issue of "similarity."*

In this instance, the subject's tendency to group objects in graphic situations predominated. Only after we reminded him that he had to select objects on the basis of "similarity" was he able to classify them categorically. The following provides an even clearer indication that some subjects operated on two planes of thought, shifting from one to the other method of classification.

Subject: Rust., age fifty-six, a *mirab* [worker assigned to distribute water from irrigation system], barely literate. Is given the series *ax-hatchet-sickle* which he is to complete by selecting from group *saw-ear of grain-log.*

"The saw fits in with the others—they're all farming tools."

**And does the ear of grain fit too?**

"These are farming tools, whereas the grain isn't, though you could reap it with the sickle."

*Categorical classification predominates, though both methods are used.*

Subject is given the series *tree-flower-ear of grain* and supplementary group (*rosebush-bird*).

"If you look at the tree, the thing next to it should be the rosebush."

**Do any of the others fit in that group?**

"Yes, the swallow. There's a tree here and a flower—a pretty spot. The swallow will sit here and sing."

*Same tendency as in preceding response.*

**If I asked you to arrange these things in some kind of order, which would you put here?**

"The rosebush. But when we line them all up in order, we can also put the swallow in."

*Same tendency again.*

**But if you have to put together things that are alike, of the same kind, would the swallow fit?**

"No, only the flowers would."

*Establishes precise categorical series.*

Subject is given the series *horse-sheep* and the alternatives (*camel-pail-house*).

"The camel goes here. The ones over here are animals."

*Immediately designates category.*

**Then the others don't fit in here?**

"Some of them do. You need the pail to water the animals."

*Lapses into concrete thinking.*

**But if you had to arrange them in some kind of order, which would you put together?**

"If you arrange them according to work, only the camel fits. The sheep doesn't fit because it's livestock—it's used for meat."

*Narrows range of concrete grouping.*

**Does the house fit in with the first group?**

"It does. If you round up all the animals you can find space for them in the house."

**But if you put them in order which one would fit with the first group?**

"The camel. You have to line up all the animals and then you can lead them into the house."

*Uses both categorical and situational thinking.*

This example clearly illustrates that some subjects had reached a transitional stage in which they used both modes of grouping: categorical, which they defined as ranking objects "in order," and situational, a supplementary measure they reverted to when trying to reason independently.

Our third group of subjects—young people who had a year or two of schooling, served in the army, or became collective-farm activists (despite their minimal amount of education)—presented an entirely different picture. These subjects had no problem classifying objects according to some abstract attribute. Although some of them tried to use situational thinking, they were sufficiently oriented toward abstract thinking to overcome the tendency. Once an abstract mode of classification was suggested, it carried over to their treatment of new groups of objects. These subjects were far less rigid and readily reconsidered various attributes that could be used as a basis for classification. The following examples are indicative of their behavior.

Subject: Yadgar, age eighteen, studied at village school in Shakhimardan for two years; employed as timekeeper on collective farm. Given the series: *glass-saucepan-spectacles-bottle.*

"The glass, spectacles, and bottle all fit together. They're made of glass but the saucepan is metal."

*Immediately classifies in categorical terms.*

**Yet one fellow told me the spectacles didn't fit here.**

"No, they're glass, while the saucepan is made of metal. I don't know why he said that."

**Think about it.**

"I'd argue with that fellow, I don't agree. These are glass things and the saucepan is metal. How can he say they're similar?"

*Continues to categorize in terms of same attribute.*

**What similarity is there between a glass, a saucepan, a bottle, and spectacles?**

"In its way each one is necessary, each does a job, but it's the three glass things here that are similar."

**Could you use one word for these things?**

"Yes, you can call them 'containers.' "

**That means the three belong together?**

*Is silent for a while.*

"No, they're not alike. These other three go together. They didn't just happen that way, they were made in a glass factory."

*With a bit of prompting, readily isolates the general concept applicable to another category but adheres to the attribute already selected.*

Subject: Sult., age twenty, barely literate; lived in Tashkent for a short time. Given the series: *hammer-saw-log-hatchet.*

"The wood doesn't fit here. Wood just lies on the ground, whereas the other three are used for different kinds of work."

*Classifies categorically though fails to use categorical term.*

**Yet some people say the hammer doesn't fit here.**

"I don't know whether that's right or not. This is a log and this is a hatchet. If the hatchet doesn't cut through, you can use the hammer to beat on it."

*Reverts to situational thinking.*

**What one word could you use for these three things?**

"You could call them tools."

**Name some other tools.**

"Plane, shovel, scissors, knife."

**Can you call a log a tool?**

"No, it's wood."

Given the series: *dagger-bird-rifle-bullet.*

"The bird doesn't fit here, it's made of feathers."

*Uses categorical classification.*

Given the series: *bottle-glass-saucepan-spectacles.*

"The spectacles don't fit here. No, it's the saucepan that doesn't. It's a metal thing, whereas the others are fine."

*Attempts to single out another attribute.*

Given the series: *tree-flower-ear of grain-bird.*

"The bird doesn't fit. The others are trees."

*Uses categorical classification.*

Similar results were obtained in the "selective" version of this experiment.

Subject: Yadgar, age eighteen, attended school for two years in village of Shakhimardan. Given the series: *ax-sickle-hatchet . . . (log-saw)*.

"The saw belongs here."

**Why?**

"These are all made of metal."

Given the series: *bush-tree . . . (rosebush-bird-house)*.

"The rosebush has to go here."

**Why?**

"Because all these are trees that grow."

Subject: Nurzev, age sixteen, attended a village school for two years. Given the series: *ax-sickle-hatchet . . . (log-saw)*.

"I'd pick the saw. All these things work, but the other doesn't. It isn't metal like the rest of the things."

Given the series: *tree-ear of grain . . . (rose-bird-house)*.

"I'd pick the rose."

At this point another subject interjects: "A tree is also a very important thing for a person. You can carry a rose in your hand but a tree brings forth fruit."

"No, a rose is a flower and so is an ear of wheat, and when a tree grows it also blossoms."

Given the series: *horse-sheep . . . (person-camel-araba)*.

"The camel goes here—these are all living things."

Subject: Rakhm., age twenty-six, attended school for two years. Given the series: *ax-sickle . . . (log-saw)*.

"I'd pick the saw. It fits with the others because they're all metal."

Given the series: *camel-sheep . . . (horse-wagon-person)*.

"I'd pick the horse, then all three will be the same—they'll all be animals."

Given the series: *tree-shrub . . . (bird-rose-house)*.

"The flower goes here. All these things grow."

We believe that this survey of the responses to the tests on classification reveals an interesting pattern. Subjects from remote villages who live almost exclusively off the land have had considerable experience working it, but are uneducated and illiterate, using a method of classification that differs radically from those we customarily employ. The procedure of isolating an attribute in order to construct an abstract category into which suitable objects can be subsumed is completely foreign to their way of thinking. Either they reject such "categorical" classification entirely or consider it a possible but irrelevant alternative.

These subjects performed operations that our experiment had not foreseen. Some of them classified objects by immediately appraising their practical value or "necessity." In doing so, they indicated the function each object performed but made no attempt to establish any closer connection between them. Others tried to think of a situation in which the objects would have some practical interrelation. Generally, such subjects reconstructed concrete situations from their daily experience. They had no hesitation grouping together a saw, an ax, and a log. As they put it, "You have to saw the log, then split it with the ax; all these things work together." Or they would remind us that "unless you have a log in the group there's no work for an ax and a saw to do." They grouped a house, a bird, and a rosebush together because a "rosebush should be near a house, while a bird can sit on the bush and sing." Some subjects even insisted that the drawings of objects be placed closer together, noting that it would "take them a lot of time to collect all these things."

Every attempt to suggest the possibility of categorical grouping met with protest: "That's wrong. Some stupid fellow told you that, he doesn't understand anything." Even when we pointed out that "similar" objects belonged in one category, these subjects were unconvinced; they interpreted the instruction to "group similar things" to mean select "necessary" or "suitable" objects. References to general terms (*asbob*—tools; *idish*—vessels) did not overcome their tendency to group objects in concretely effective ways. They either disregarded generic terms or considered them irrelevant, in no way essential to the business of classification. Clearly, different psychological processes determined their manner of grouping which hinged on concrete, situational thinking rather than abstract operations which entail the generalizing function of language.

There was a marked difference between these subjects and a second, intermediate group composed of people who had taken some courses or worked on a collective farm (among collective-farm activists). Though these subjects were inclined to use situational thinking, it was relatively simple for them to shift to verbal and logical operations and classify objects in terms of a specific category. On the other hand, they had a far from solid grasp of categorical thinking. As they proceeded to work out a problem independently, they quickly lapsed into visual thinking which, in their minds, provided an alternative to abstract classification and frequently took precedence over the latter.

A third group of subjects, primarily young people who had been systematically trained in school for a year or two, differed significantly from the first two groups. They chiefly employed theoretical operations which required verbal and logical thinking; the task of isolating a particular attribute as a basis for categorization seemed to them a natural, self-evident procedure. Table 7 makes the differences between the groups apparent.

Clearly, the latter two groups had no trouble shifting from graphic, functional modes of generalization to abstract, categorical classification. A minimal amount of education and work on a collective farm—which entails organized contact with people, group discussions of economic problems, and participation in communal life—was sufficient to induce fundamental changes in their habits of thought. They were

Table 7. Groupings and Classifications

| Group | Number of subjects | Graphic method of grouping | Graphic and categorical methods of grouping | Categorical classification |
|---|---|---|---|---|
| Illiterate peasants from remote villages | 26 | 21 (80%) | 4 (16%) | 1 (4%) |
| Collective-farm activists (barely literate) | 10 | 0 | 3 (30%) | 7 (70%) |
| Young people with one to two years' schooling | 12 | 0 | 0 | 12 (100%) |

able to grasp the principle of theoretical operations that had previously been incomprehensible because they played no effective role in these people's lives.

We wish to stress the principal facts derived from the tests described thus far.

(1) The main group of subjects classified objects not according to verbal and logical principles, but according to practical schemes. Nonetheless, such concrete thinking is neither innate nor genetically determined. It results from illiteracy and the rudimentary types of activity that have prevailed in these subjects' daily experience. When the pattern of their lives changes and the range of their experience broadens, when they learn to read and write, to become part of a more advanced culture, the greater complexity of their activity stimulates new ideas. These changes, in turn, bring about a radical reorganization of their habits of thinking, so that they learn to use and appreciate the value of theoretical procedures that formerly seemed irrelevant.

(2) As we have noted, subjects were asked to group objects that were "similar," had common characteristics. What we had yet to clarify was whether they interpreted the word "similar" as we did or whether it meant different things to different groups of subjects. We had repeatedly observed that some subjects disregarded the word or construed it to mean "applicable to a general situation" (even though Uzbek has a specific term for the latter). For these subjects, generic terms such as "tools" or "vessels" also did not seem to have the same "categorical" meaning they do in a system of abstract thought.

Consequently, we had to devise special tests to ascertain the following. To what extent did our subjects use concrete thinking to perform precisely those elementary logical operations that are by nature abstract and categorical? What did the generic terms they used to group objects actually mean to them? Did their usage of these terms correspond to ours or was it significantly different?

**Tests on the Detection of Similarity**

The ability to detect similarity is a primary, integral part of the process of classifying objects. The simplest type of abstraction consists of comparing two objects and determining a resemblance between them.

As such, it presupposes an ability to isolate (abstract) a common feature of both objects as a basis of comparison. Given the simplicity of the operation, experiments on comparison and generalization have become a standard part of research studies on concept formation.

The classical studies of Binet and other psychologists proved long ago that a person can detect differences in objects long before he can establish a basis of similarity among them. The reason for this is perfectly obvious. In order to discern how two contrasting objects differ, one need only describe their physical attributes; hence, the whole procedure hinges on immediate impressions or visual memory. On the other hand, it is far more difficult to establish a resemblance between objects (particularly when this is not apparent from immediate impressions). Insofar as it implies an ability to isolate and compare attributes, such a procedure inevitably includes certain verbal and logical components.

Since we wished to determine whether our subjects' approach to comparison and generalization (that is, the detection of similarity) involved linguistic and logical distinctions, we had them compare: (a) objects that were clearly dissimilar; and (b) those that were difficult to incorporate in practical schemes. In both instances, subjects' immediate impressions prompted them to delineate dissimilar features. In order to detect the covert similarity of these objects (generally their categorical relationship), subjects had to disregard the strikingly dissimilar physical features of the two and not attempt to visualize different situations in which each could function. Typical examples of the objects we asked them to compare were the following: a cucumber and a rose; a crow and a fish; a horse and a man; a landowner and a farmhand.

When subjects confined their responses to a description of the physical differences they observed, we tried to facilitate the task by proposing some term of generalization. Since we did not want to disclose the actual basis of similarity, however, we kept it hidden in a rather oblique way, pointing out that in Chinese one word (invented, of course) designated both objects. We asked our subjects why they thought the Chinese used such a term and what it could possibly mean. The experiments were conducted with a sizeable number of subjects who, in background and training, corresponded to the groups of participants in the experiments on classification.

There was a huge difference between the results of this series of experiments and those one usually obtains from adults who have had some education or acquired a modicum of culture. The latter have no problem comparing two objects and, on the basis of their similarity, assigning them to a general category (a cucumber and a rose represent plant life; a crow and a fish, animal life). With our subjects—that is, our first group (illiterate peasants)—the procedure took quite a different turn. At times they merely described each of the objects, insisting that the two had nothing in common. They would provide a detailed account of the purposes they served, the situations in which they were usually encountered, or try to establish some closer connection between them by imagining a concrete instance in which the two interacted. In some instances they tried to think of a situation in which both objects performed identical operations, thereby assuming they could establish a functional basis of similarity. Another approach—one wholly irrelevant to the job of categorization—was to determine some physical resemblance between the two objects.

For the most part, subjects refused to consider why the objects we had asked them to compare ("such different things") could be designated by one term in Chinese. (The reference to "Chinese" usage was utterly unconvincing.) Only after we explained in detail how the two objects pertained to a single category did they accept the idea—at least, ostensibly. In trying to think through a problem, they continued to stress the dissimilarities of the two objects, pointing out that it was impossible to group them both in one situation. In this respect, the data presented much the same pattern as the results of the preceding experiments.

Subject: Maksud, age thirty-eight, illiterate, works in Lalazar region.

**What do a chicken and a dog have in common?**

"They're not alike. A chicken has two legs, a dog has four. A chicken has wings but a dog doesn't. A dog has big ears and a chicken's are small."

*Describes differences rather than similarities.*

**You've told me what is different about them. How are they alike?**

"They're not alike at all."

**Is there one word you could use for them both?**

"No, of course not."

**What word fits both a chicken and a dog?**

"I don't know."

**Would the word "animal" fit?**

"Yes."

*Accepts term of generalization.*

**What do a fish and a crow have in common?**

"A fish—it lives in the water. A crow flies. If the fish just lays on top of the water, the crow could peck at it. A crow can eat a fish but a fish can't eat a crow."

*Exhibits no carryover to next pair of objects; makes no effort to determine similarity and instead includes objects in a general situation.*

**Could you use one word for them both?**

"If you call them animals, that wouldn't be right. A fish isn't an animal and a crow isn't either. A crow can eat a fish but a fish can't eat a bird. A person can eat a fish but not a crow."

*Unable to find common term: reverts to description of differences.*


Subject: Sakhumb, age thirty-four, peasant from village of Yardan, illiterate.

**What do blood and water have in common?**

"What's alike about them is that water washes off all sorts of dirt, so it can wash off blood too."

*Indicates interaction, not similarity, of objects.*

**What do a crow and a fish have in common?**

"There's lots of differences between a crow and a fish. One lives in the water, the other flies. The only way they're alike is that a fish uses the water and a crow does sometimes—when it gets thirsty."

*Refers to common functions to try and establish closer connection between objects.*

**What do a mountain and a poplar have in common?**

"A poplar needs water to grow, but God made the mountains. That's how they come to be standing there."

*Points out differences.*

**But what likeness is there between them?**

"There's no likeness. We've lived in these mountains a long time and never seen any likeness between those things. [Looks up at the mountains and at a poplar and shakes his head negatively.]

**Could you say that mountains and a poplar are both tall?**

"Mountains are very big, but a poplar's small. In some places they're level, but mountains are huge and a poplar's small. I'm looking at them now and I don't see any likeness at all."

*Refuses to try and detect similarity.*

Subject: Khadzhy Mar., age forty-five, peasant from village of Yardan, illiterate.

**What do mountains and a poplar have in common?**

"Mountains—these are mountains. But a poplar grows because it drinks water. If we plant a poplar on a mountain, it won't grow. It needs good soil."

*Tries to link objects in one situation.*

**In what way are they alike?**

"If you look at them from far off, the mountains are huge, whereas the poplar's small."

**But what likeness is there?**

"There's a little bit, seeing a poplar's also tall."

**What do a rose and a cucumber have in common?**

"What's alike about them is that they grow. When the cucumber grows, it blooms and so does the rose. Except that the rose stays like it is, whereas the cucumber turns into a fruit you can eat."

*Cites common physical feature—both objects "blossom."*

**What do a landowner and a farmhand have in common?**

"There's a huge difference between them. What a landowner's been able to get for himself, the farmhands never have."

**What likeness is there between them?**

"What's alike is that a landowner has got something and a farmhand hasn't. When a landowner wants to eat, he eats, but when a farmhand wants to eat, he first has to go to the landowner."

*Indicates differences.*

**But what do they have in common?**

"A landowner's walked the same roads a farmhand has, but what the landowner's been able to do, the farmhand hasn't. A landowner talks and so does a farmhand, but a farmhand does what the landowner tells him to."

*Uses graphic situations to try and determine similar features but merely cites interaction of the pair.*

These few examples will suffice, since they typify the approach used by our main group of subjects. Their responses indicate that when faced with the job of having to compare conflicting objects, these subjects operated almost exclusively in graphic terms. In one instance a subject made no attempt to relate the two objects to a general, abstract category. In another, he tried—somewhere along the line—to think of an abstract category but instead visualized a situation in which both objects performed the same function. ("A landowner walks and a farmhand walks; a cucumber grows and a rose grows.") Some subjects searched for common physical features. ("When a cucumber blossoms it's like a flower and a rose is also a flower.") Another approach was to cite concrete interrelationships between the two objects. ("A crow can peck at a fish." "A poplar can grow on a mountain.")

The task of comparing two objects and establishing a basis of similarity presented no problem for our second group of subjects, despite their negligible amount of education. They readily assigned both objects to a single category, even though each could be visualized in completely different situations.

**Tests on the Definition of Concepts**

To define a concept by classifying a specific object, phenomenon, or activity within a larger category amounts to one of the most elementary operations of abstract thought. As we know from standard psychological experiments, the definition of a concept is a clear-cut verbal and logical operation in which one uses a series of logically subordinate ideas to arrive at a general conclusion, automatically disregarding all extralogical considerations. A person who defines an apple tree as a tree and a goat as an animal disregards the attributes peculiar to an apple tree or a goat and isolates some essential quality of each that pertains to a generic category.

We are also well aware that one develops an ability to formulate concepts primarily through education, through mastering certain principles of thought. Vygotsky explored two classes of concepts—"academic" and "mundane." An elementary-school pupil can easily learn to define the former, even though at first he fails to establish any connection between these and events in his daily life. On the other hand, despite his considerable fund of practical experience, he finds it far more difficult to define "mundane" concepts, since they play no role in his academic life. To the extent that he acquires a body of systematic information, he begins to discern a closer relationship between the two types of concepts. An adolescent or an adult with some degree of education tends increasingly to evaluate—and integrate—mundane and academic concepts, to categorize the former and then define them within some broader conceptual scheme.

Considering that our subjects thought in practical rather than theoretical terms, substituting graphic operations for verbal and logical procedures, we were curious to observe how they would define concepts. What psychological features would they exhibit? What progression of thought would their responses indicate? Would they have any premises to guide them in defining concepts in theoretical terms?

Research on the psychological aspect of the definition of concepts would be of great value in educational psychology and warrants special investigation. Since this was simply a supplementary part of our project, we will not discuss it at length but merely consider the most salient data our experiment yielded.

On the one hand, we wanted to observe how subjects defined commonly used objects ("mundane" concepts); on the other, abstract ideas inculcated by the social system ("academic" concepts). "Tree," "sun," "automobile," and such were examples of the former; "a cooperative," "freedom"—instances of the latter. Generally we questioned subjects about these in the course of conversation. Moreover, since many of the subjects had had no experience "defining concepts," we devised a hypothetical situation that would make the task appear more meaningful. We asked them to consider how they would explain a particular object or word to someone who had never encountered these, had no idea what they signified.

In conducting the experiment, we focused primarily on the methods our subjects used to try and define concepts. Of the twenty-two subjects who participated, eleven were completely illiterate; the others had a negligible amount of education (a year or two) and some experience of collective work. The responses were so uniform that there was no need to consider a broader sample.

For the most part, our first group of subjects (illiterate peasants from outlying villages) refused to define a given concept, insisting that it was senseless to "define" or "talk about" things that were perfectly obvious. "The sun is the sun, everyone knows that." "There are cars everywhere, so people know what they are." They claimed that if a person had no idea what such things were the only alternative was to have him see for himself. When we tried to elicit some kind of definition, they usually responded with tautologies: "A car is a car." In some cases they told us how it operated, pointed out its functions, described its appearance—its physical attributes. Only when they became somewhat more skillful at the task did they realize that they could help clarify the nature of one object by comparing it with a second. Yet in doing so, they performed precisely the same operations they used in the experiments on comparison and contrast. Hence, their attempts to define mundane and academic concepts were limited to descriptions of basic attributes or practical functions.

Subject: Illi-Khodzh., age twenty-two, peasant from remote village, illiterate.

**Try to explain to me what a tree is.**

"Why should I? Everyone knows what a tree is, they don't need me telling them."

*Rejects need for explanation.*

**Still, try and explain it.**

"There are trees here everywhere; you won't find a place that doesn't have trees. So what's the point of my explaining?"

**But some people have never seen trees, so you might have to explain.**

"Okay. You say there are no trees where these people come from. So I'll tell them how we plant beetroots by using seeds, how the root goes into the earth and the leaves come out on top. That's the way we plant a tree, the roots go down . . . "

*Tries to explain by pointing out distinct features of object.*

**How would you define a tree in two words?**

"In two words? Apple tree, elm, poplar."

*Enumerates instead of defining.*

**What is a car? Can you explain it to me?**

"It uses fire for its power and a person drives it. If it has no oil and no one to drive it, it won't move."

*Attempts to define object by citing its features.*

**How would you explain a car to someone who had never seen one?**

"Everyone knows what a car is, there are cars all over the world. There's so many cars it just can't be people have never seen them."

*Rejects hypothetical instance.*

**Say you go to a place where there are no cars. What will you tell people?**

"If I go, I'll tell them that buses have four legs, chairs in front for people to sit on, a roof for shade and an engine. But when you get right down to it, I'd say: 'If you get in a car and go for a drive, you'll find out.' "

*First tries to define object through graphic description, then insists on the need for firsthand experience.*

Subject: Akhmet., age forty-four, Kirghiz from remote village, illiterate.

**Tell me, what is a car?**

"When it screeches, goes screaming down the road, moves this way and that, and has fire burning inside it . . . "

*Describes physical aspects.*

**Would a person understand you if he'd never seen a car?**

"If he goes for a drive in one, he'll see for himself. If you'd never seen these mountains and I started to tell you they're great big mountains with snow on them—why, you'd never understand. If a person hasn't seen a thing, he won't be able to understand it. And that's that."

*Refuses to attempt definition.*

**What is the sun?**

"If a person's blind and I tell him the sun's come up, it's overhead, it keeps us warm—he won't understand. What else can I tell him? I've never seen the sun up close, so how can I say what it is?"

*Enumerates attributes. Refuses to define object he hasn't "seen up close."*

In the above instances subjects did one of two things. They either refused to define an object they had never "seen," "got a close look at," or replaced definitions with detailed descriptions of physical attributes.

Subjects in the second group tried to arrive at a definition by means of comparison. (These were people who had had a minimal amount of education or some systematic contact with people through their work.) The following exemplify their responses.

Subject: Nurmal, eighteen-year-old girl from outlying village; had taken courses designed to overcome illiteracy but was barely able to read and write.

**What is a car?**

"A car? It's called a car, and a kukushka [dinkey] is a kukushka.

**But try and explain it.**

"It's smaller than a room, uses fire, and people sit in it . . . There are also small cars, and kukushkas and buses."

*Tries to define object by enumerating other objects in same category.*

**Name some other things that are like them.**

"Cab drivers, bicycles, trains . . . I've told you all the things I've seen."

*Uses somewhat different attempt to define concept.*

**What is freedom?**

"I've heard that women have got their freedom, but that's all I know. It means that the landowners oppressed them before but now they've escaped from their misery."

Subject: Aziz, age thirty-six, works in the Mikhnat farm; has completed a ten-week agricultural course.

**What is a car?**

"A car is a thing that moves fast, uses electricity, water, and air. It covers great distances so it makes difficult work easier."

*Defines by singling out most essential features of object.*

**What is the sun?**

"The night is dark, while in the day the sun lights up the world, so everyone benefits from it."

**What is the best way to define the sun?**

"To explain it, you have to compare it—there's no other way. That's why I brought in the night."

*Uses comparison and contrast to attempt definition.*

**What is a cooperative?**

"The shops used to be run by the landowners and the merchants. They sold goods to the peasants for high prices. Now the government has organized its own shops—a cooperative. The peasants can buy goods there cheaply. A cooperative makes a person part of the community, it provides for the people."

*Defines in far more detail concept introduced by the social system; makes greater use of abstract categories; clarifies one concept by means of another.*

Subject: Isamutd., age thirty-four, worker in the Mikhnat farm; has taken courses designed to overcome illiteracy.

**What is the sun? How would you describe it to a blind man?**

"I'd say it rises in the morning and sets in the evening. I don't know how I'd explain it to him, can't even think how . . . All I could tell him is that when it rises, its rays give warmth to growing things and strengthen the crops."

*Tries to define by citing important features of object.*

**What is a car?**

"If someone asks me I'd say it makes work easier. If you don't have any flour or firewood, a car can get them to you very quickly."

*Same approach.*

**How would you explain a car to someone who had never seen one?**

"It looks like an araba [kind of bullock cart], only an araba is a simple thing whereas a car has a complicated build. It's not something a person can make for himself. It takes a lot of learning to make, comes from a factory."

*Uses comparison to clarify definition.*

**What is a cooperative?**

"If someone asks me what a cooperative is, I'd say it's a state warehouse with goods and clothes, so it prevents all kinds of shortages."

*Defines concept through its essential function and relation to another concept ("warehouse").*

One can see that entirely different psychological processes governed the responses of these subjects. Unlike the first group, they did not repudiate the task but tried to define an object logically by comparing it with another. Although they were unable to assign everyday objects to logical categories, in defining "academic" concepts (a cooperative, for example) they used a more complex approach, analyzing the origin and social significance of the concept and, in some cases, categorizing it.

Our third group of subjects (collective-farm activists or people with somewhat more education than the second group) exhibited a still more complex approach. They defined social concepts in greater detail —often by using other abstract (categorical) phenomena as a basis of comparison.

Subject: Badoub, age thirty, literate collective-farm worker, had taken some short courses.

**What is the sun?**

"Is it possible a person has never seen the sun? Only someone who dies the moment he's born. How can I describe it? The sun gives light to the world. A person can't live without the sun, he'd die if it weren't for it."

*Defines concept by citing essential attributes.*

**What is a car?**

"It's made in a factory. In one trip it can cover the distance it would take a horse ten to make—it moves that fast. It uses fire and steam. We first have to set the fire going so the water gets steaming hot—the steam gives the machine its power . . . I don't know whether there is water in a car, must be. But water isn't enough, it also needs fire."

*Defines object by describing its structure and operations.*

**What is a cooperative?**

"It makes us part of the community. It's our industry. You see, some shopkeepers charge ten rubles for a thing that's worth one, whereas a cooperative takes the cotton we produce and sells it cheaply."

*Defines concept by describing its purpose and by citing other abstract concepts to which it relates.*

The responses from all three groups offer sufficient evidence for fairly clear-cut conclusions. Illiterate subjects, who have had no experience of communal work, either refuse to provide a verbal definition of objects or do so by way of detailed, graphic descriptions. On the other hand, subjects who are culturally more advanced, have acquired some education, and become involved in systematic collective work (which requires effective communication) develop other means of defining concepts. Although their manner of thinking is primarily graphic-functional, not theoretical, they do at least try to define concepts, using comparison and contrast to detail the various features of objects pertaining to a given class. It is worth noting that, even at this stage, subjects are better able to define social than "mundane" concepts and to categorize the former.

Subjects with considerably more experience of collective work and a somewhat better education are capable of defining a significantly greater number of concepts. They analyze the nature of an object in detail and, at times, perceive its relation to other concepts. This type of analysis also carries over to their definition of mundane concepts. The subjects we examined were not sufficiently developed culturally to provide "succinct" definitions by thinking in terms of broader conceptual schemes. Nonetheless, the fact that they could make the transition from a graphic, situational mode of thought to the elementary stages of conceptual thinking is of paramount importance.

### The Meaning of Generic Terms

Our research indicated that at a certain stage in the development of cognitive processes, people do not employ verbal and logical methods to group objects but reconstruct graphic situations in which the latter can function. Consequently, in this mode of thought the primary function of language is not to formulate abstractions and generalizations about categorical relationships but to revive suitably graphic, practical situations.

We wanted to clarify several questions about our subjects' use of language. Had their predominantly visual type of thinking altered the meaning of the generic terms used in abstract thought? That is, did they attach a far more concrete meaning to some of the terms that have acquired general, categorical significance for us? The latter supposition fully accords with Vygotsky's idea that the meaning of words changes in the course of cognitive development. Psychology could benefit from additional data in support of his hypothesis which, given some of the facts we have described, strikes us as entirely sound. As we have noted, subjects repeatedly construed the word "similar"—which has a precise lexical meaning—to imply "suitable" or "appropriate," using it to designate objects that applied to a given situation. They felt no constraint about saying that a log and an ax were similar, meaning that the two "fit together." Thus, were we able to corroborate our suppositions about their use of language, we would clarify an aspect of semantics not generally reflected in dictionaries but only in various historical stages of linguistic usage.

We were also curious to learn whether our subjects would give a different meaning to words such as "tools" or "vessels." This point required special verification, since many of the practical group arrangements our subjects compiled did not contradict the general concepts they formulated for them. Rather, it appeared that such concepts pertained to abstract categories, not to concrete interrelations of the objects.

Through our analysis we hoped to get a better understanding of the following. Did the facts we observed reflect sheer disregard for the meaning of words (which, in the instances referred to, was equivalent to their denotations)? Had practical considerations come to outweigh meaning for these people? Or did the facts have deeper implications—namely, that practical experience had altered the very meaning of words, that what we were dealing with here was a different scheme of semantics?

In the special experiments designed to clarify these points, we used extremely simple devices. We asked subjects who had participated in the experiment on classification whether the groups of objects they had compiled could be designated by an appropriate generic term ("tools," "instruments," "vessels," and so forth). If they answered affirmatively, we asked them to specify other objects which the word designated, or select them from a supplementary group that we presented. (In some cases the latter corresponded to the same category of objects; in others, only to their practical interrelationships.) During the course of the experiment, we questioned subjects at length in order to clarify the meaning they invested in a given generic term.

Of the fifteen people who participated in the experiment, ten represented our main group of subjects (illiterate peasants). The others were selected from the group that had only a negligible amount of education but were actively involved in communal work. The results of these experiments confirmed our supposition about a change in the meaning of words, though this may appear unlikely from the initial responses we obtained.

The majority of subjects in our first group considered the definition of a word an irrelevant procedure which they immediately replaced by visual thinking, incorporating the designated object into a practical scheme. In their case, the "meaning" of the word had acquired an "overgrowth" of graphic-functional connotations. This in no way stripped the word of the meaning customarily attached to it; nonetheless, from a psychological standpoint, these subjects used the word in a decidedly atypical way. Some of them had no hesitation about applying a generalizing term to a concrete situation; others first pointed out the specific ways in which objects interacted, thereby indicating that in their minds the principle of utility had obscured the primary meaning of generic terms.

Additional psycholinguistic studies would be needed to corroborate this observation which, we believe, is sufficiently noteworthy to warrant consideration by specialists. Cited below are some of the responses we obtained in this part of our study.

Participants: Kar. Farfil., age twenty-five, peasant from the village of Palman (I); Yarb. Madmar, age thirty-two (II); Mad., age twenty-six, drayman (III). All three subjects, illiterate, were shown drawings of *saw-ax-hammer.*

**Would you say these things are tools?**

All three subjects: "Yes."

**What about a log?**

I.    "It also belongs with these. We make all sorts of things out of logs —handles, doors, and the handles of tools."

II.   "We say a log is a tool because it works with tools to make things. The pieces of logs go into making tools."

**But one man said a log isn't a tool since it can't saw or chop.**

III.  "Some crazy fellow must have told you that! After all, you need a log for tools . . . together with iron it can cut."

*Subjects include in the concept of "tools" objects from which they are made.*

**But I can't call wood a tool!**

III. "Yes, you can—you can make handles out of it."

**But can you really say wood is a tool?**

II. "It is! Poles are made out of it, handles . . . We call all the things we have need of 'tools.' "

*Principle of necessity determines use of word "tools."*

**Name all the tools you can.**

III. "An ax, a mosque [light carriage on springs], and also the tree we tether a horse to if there's no pole around. Look, if we didn't have this board here, we wouldn't be able to keep the water in this irrigation ditch. So that's also a tool, and so is the wood that goes to make a blackboard."

*Same principle applies.*

**Name all the tools used to produce things.**

I. "We have a saying: take a look in the fields and you'll see tools."

*Attaches broader meaning to the word "tool."*

III. "Hatchet, ax, saw, yoke harness, and the thong used in a saddle."

**Can you really call wood a tool?**

II. "Yes, of course! If we have no wood to use with an ax, we can't plow and we can't build a carriage."

Subject: Nazir Said, age twenty-seven, illiterate peasant from Yukhar Makhalla. Selects a hammer, saw, log, and hatchet and calls them "asbob."

**Can you really call a log an asbob?**

"You could but not these days, since the others have all gotten to be tools, while the log's used for making doors."

*Groups together tools and materials.*

Subject: Mirza Shiral., age fifty-seven, peasant from village of Yardan, barely literate. Groups together a hammer, saw, log, and hatchet and calls them "asbob."

**What other things do you call tools?**

"An ax, a hatchet, a saw, two men with a saw—they're all tools."

**Can you really call people tools?**

"No, but all life comes down to one thing: people join together to work."

**Can you call a log a tool?**

"Yes. All these things belong here. If you use the ax to chop the log, it will split."

*Applies the term to objects that function together to perform a job.*

**But if I split the log with my hands, could I call my hands a tool?**

"Yes, of course! They've got power and it's with this power that we split wood."

**What else can you call a tool?**

"A tractor, bulls with an ax, grain—we can nourish ourselves with it. Everything that goes into our stomachs is a tool. First a man uses his strength to plant a seed, then it grows, and then we eat the grain that ripens."

*Includes in concept both tools and their products.*


Subject: Khaid, age forty-eight, illiterate Kirghiz from Mashalyana. Groups together a hammer, saw, log, hatchet and terms them "as-bob."

**What other things can you call tools?**

"An ax, a saw, a knife, a razor, an awl."

**Can you call the string you thread an awl with a tool?**

"Yes, because it's used for things."

*Includes in concept a broad range of accessory items.*

**Is a donkey a tool?**

"Yes, because you need him for traveling."

**And firewood?**

"Of course! Firewood's the most important tool. This [picks up a clump of manure] is also a tool, because I can light a fire with it."

**Name some other tools.**

"Cocoons, they're also necessary; land—that's the most important tool. Grass, rope, a skullcap—to protect you from the heat, a head, a person—we're all things that live."

*Extends range of complex.*

Subject: Mirzab, age thirty-nine, peasant from Kizil-Kiya; studied independently but barely able to read and write. Groups together glass, saucepan, bottle, spectacles, and calls them *muim* [household objects].

**Can you call spectacles muim?**

"Yes."

**What else can you call muim?**

"Spoons, saucepans, and other things. I don't wear spectacles but other people do, so it means they're useful."

*Makes "utility" the principle of generalization.*

**Can you call fire muim?**

"Yes, of course! Without it you can't cook anything."

**How about soup?**

"Yes, you can make soup in a saucepan."

*Groups household objects with cooking vessels.*

Subject introduces another word—*idish*—which signifies cooking vessels and is asked to explain usage.

"If a bottle has vodka in it, I wouldn't say it belongs with the other things, but if it's got water, I would. The spectacles also fit with these things—you need them if your eyes are bothering you."

*Again groups in terms of principle of "utility."*

**Could you call firewood idish?**

[Thinks for a while.] "Yes, people need it to cook, need it for the vessels they cook in."

**Still, can you call it idish?**

"I don't know . . . firewood is used in many different ways for cooking food."

**Could you call soup idish?**

"I don't know whether it's an idish or not."

*Exhibits some hesitation about such a broad interpretation of the term.*

Subject: Dusmat., age thirty, illiterate, formerly a farmhand, now works in a quarry. Groups together a hammer, saw, log, and hatchet, calling them "asbob."

**What other things would you call asbob?**

"A pick, a shovel, a crowbar, a drill, a hammer."

**Could you call a board asbob?**

"Yes."

**And a log?**

"Yes, it's the most important one. If something breaks down in a wagon and you don't have some wood handy, you're in for trouble."

**And is coal asbob?**

"Of course, you can't mix cement without it."

**How about a person?**

"A person is too . . . if his stomach is empty, he can't work."

**What sort of things can you call idish [cooking vessels]?**

"A plate, a mess kit, a mug, a pail, and the water you need for it."

**But is water really idish?**

"Yes . . . No! It flows. If a container has a hole in it, water will run out."

*Reverts to inclusion of objects that function with cooking vessels but then narrows down the group.*

**What other things can you call idish?**

"A cup, a plate."

**How about firewood?**

"It's also necessary but it's not an idish."

**What about fire?**

"No. When you light it yourself, it's an idish but otherwise it isn't."

**How about matches?**

"Yes, of course. Say you've got a long ways to walk and you've got some tobacco and cigarette papers with you but no matches—how're you going to get hold of them? You need them, so they're also an idish."

*Again employs idea of "necessity."*

**But is everything that's needed an idish?**

"No, there are also asbob. I'm talking about necessary things."

These responses are remarkable. They indicate that in attempting to define the abstract, categorical meaning of a given term, subjects began by enumerating items that did in fact pertain to the designated category. Nonetheless, they soon exceeded its limits, including objects that are simply encountered together or that can be considered useful.

Further research will have to determine whether such behavior merely reflects a reversion to situational thinking or whether the meaning of a generic term in this mode of thought has an indeterminate semantic range, one that allows for the inclusion of objects that cannot be subsumed under a specific category but have some practical assocation with it. We believe the facts substantiate the latter conclusion. Judging by our subjects' responses, a word retains its primary lexical meaning but has connotations broad enough to apply not only to a specific group of objects but also to those that are related to it in actual practice.

Such linguistic phenomena were apparent only in the responses of our first group of subjects. Our second group did not attach such a broad interpretation to generic terms but used them with precise categorical meaning.

The material we examined demonstrates the modes of generalizations that typify the thinking of people who have been shaped by social, economic, and cultural conditions unlike our own. The evidence assembled indicates that the processes used to render abstractions and generalizations does not assume an invariable form at all stages of mental growth. Such processes are themselves a product of socioeconomic and cultural development.

The majority of our subjects were members of a society in which rudimentary practical functions constituted the fundamental human activity. Lacking the formal education that would have allowed for systematic intellectual development, these people regarded the logical procedures of categorization as irrelevant, of no practical value. Hence they substituted procedures that were more meaningful to them, analyzing an object according to its relevance to a functional situation. This approach took precedence over the verbal logical operations typical of abstract thinking, so that these people were inclined to use concrete thinking to reconstruct situations that could become a basis for unifying discrete objects.

The semantic and psychological structure of this mode of thinking is unique. Words have entirely different functions than they do in a system of abstract thought; they are not used to codify objects in conceptual schemes but to establish the practical interrelationship of those objects.

This mode of thought, however, undergoes a radical transformation once the conditions of people's lives change. When they acquire some education and participate in collective discussions of vital social issues, they can readily make the transition to abstract thinking. The acquisition of new experience and new ideas imparts added meaning to their use of language so that words become the principal agent of abstraction and generalization. At this point people dispense with graphic thinking and codify ideas primarily through conceptual schemes.

Naturally, in making the transition from concrete to theoretical thinking, people do not immediately acquire an ability to formulate their ideas succinctly. They exhibit much the same tendency to discursiveness that characterized their previous habits of thought. In the course of time, however, they overcome the inclination to think in visual terms and can render abstractions in a more sophisticated manner.

Education, which radically alters the nature of cognitive activity, greatly facilitates the transition from practical to theoretical operations. Once people acquire education, they make increasingly greater use of categorization to express ideas that objectively reflect reality.

An historical analysis of the specific cultural conditions that determine various methods of abstraction and generalization is of crucial importance to psychology. Such an analysis indicates that it is time we reexamined the age-old philosophical and psychological notions about the invariability of fundamental categories of thought.

# 4

## Deduction
## and Inference

We have described processes of graphic-functional generalization typical of people in a certain socioeconomic system. We have attempted to analyze the psychological structure of these processes and the structural shifts that occur when the forms of activity of these people are restructured. What is the nature of discursive, logical thinking at this stage of graphic and functional forms of reflection of reality?

### THE PROBLEM

Conceptual thinking involves an enormous expansion of the resultant forms of cognitive activity. A person capable of abstract thought reflects the external world more profoundly and completely and makes conclusions and inferences from perceived phenomena on the basis not only of his personal experience but also of schemes of logical thinking that objectively take shape in a fairly advanced stage of development of cognitive activity.

The appearance of verbal and logical codes enabling one to abstract the essential features of objects and thus assign these objects to general categories leads to the formation of a more complex logical apparatus. This apparatus permits conclusions to be drawn from given premises without having to resort to immediate graphic-functional experience, and make it possible to acquire new knowledge in a discursive and verbal-logical fashion. This is what provided the transition from sensory to rational consciousness, a phenomenon that the classics of Marxism regarded as one of the most important in history.

The presence of general concepts to which more particular ones are hierarchically subordinate creates a logical system of codes. This code makes it possible to change from one class of things to another and creates a system of verbal and logical relations through which human concepts are channeled. As theoretical thought develops, the system becomes more and more complex. In addition to words (more precisely, meanings, which have a complex conceptual structure) and sentences (whose logical and grammatical structure permit them to function as the basic apparatus of judgments), this system also includes more complex verbal and logical "devices" that make it possible to perform the operations of deduction and inference without reliance on direct experience.

One of the objective devices that arises in the process of the development of cognitive activity is the syllogism—a set of individual judgments of varying degrees of generality in certain objectively necessary relationships to one another. Two sentences, of which the first ("precious metals do not rust") is in the nature of a general judgment and comprises the "major premise," while the second ("gold is a precious metal") is a particular proposition and comprises the "minor premise," are not perceived by the developed consciousness as two isolated phrases in juxtaposition. A human being whose theoretical thought processes are well developed will perceive these as a completed logical relation implying the conclusion, "Hence gold does not rust." This conclusion does not require any personal experience; it is arrived at through a syllogism created objectively by historical experience. A considerable proportion of our intellectual operations involve such verbal and logical systems; they comprise the basic network of codes along which the connections in discursive human thought are channeled.

The basic nature of these logical schemas is so obvious that many psychologists (for example, phenomenologists or adherents of the Würzburg school) were inclined to regard them as basic properties of human consciousness and spoke about "logical feelings," assuming implicitly that they exist in the same forms at all stages of history.

Piaget was the first to entertain doubts. In his well-known studies of the ontogenesis of intellectual operations, he showed that the basic processes of logical thought, in the form of induction and deduction, are a result of development and that in the earlier stages of children's cognitive activity these logical processes are replaced by less sophisticated forms of "transduction," in which direct impressions play a much greater part than the as-yet-underdeveloped verbal and logical schemas.

A great many studies appeared after Piaget's classic investigations, and they came to comprise a new field of science: genetic logic. This field claimed that the notion that logical categories are universal and constant is incorrect and that the "logical schemas" earlier regarded as basic and constant forms of conscious existence were in fact the result of a complex psychological development.

But these assertions needed to be developed and checked. Are the above logical schemas invariant at different stages of social and historical development? Do they have the same form in productive thinking processes in different cultures? Are they equally engaged in concrete thinking processes in successive phases of cultural development? What exactly is the structure of derivational and inferential processes among people whose life rests upon concrete practical activity? Special experiments were required to answer these questions.

## EXPERIMENTS WITH SYLLOGISMS

Our first experiments were intended to show how the process of inference from syllogisms occurred for our subjects. We were interested in how they would use the syllogism procedure, as the simplest model of discursive operations; how the logical relations of the constituent parts of the syllogism would function in their thinking; and how the operation of theoretical inference from the relationship between the major and minor premise would interact with the conclusions they drew from immediate experience.

### Procedure

The subjects were presented with a complete syllogism, including the major and minor premise. Then they were asked to repeat the entire system, to determine if they had perceived the components as part of a single logical schema or as isolated judgments. Particular attention was paid to the distortions of the premises and questions that occurred on repetition. These distortions could provide a reliable criterion of the extent to which the syllogisms were perceived as a unified system.

After repetition of the syllogism, we attempted to see if the premises could be used to make the appropriate deduction. The syllogism was corrected (if errors had been made in repeating it) and the subject was asked to provide an answer on his own to the question completing the syllogism. So that the basis on which a particular judgment was made could become clear, the subject was asked to explain why he had arrived at the particular conclusion.

To determine if judgment were made on the basis of the logic of the major and minor premises or were derived from the subject's own practical experience, all syllogisms were divided into two parts. One part consisted of syllogisms whose content was taken from the subject's immediate practical experience. The other syllogisms had content divorced from such experience. In the latter case inferences could be made only by logical deduction.

Twenty subjects took part in the experiments, of whom fifteen were peasants from remote regions who had spent little time in large cities and who had no education. As in the earlier series, there was a comparison group of five collective-farm activists and young people who had received short-term (one or two years) school education. (The data obtained from the comparison group were so uniform that enlarging it any further seemed pointless.)

## Repetition of Syllogisms

Subjects with well-established forms of theoretical thinking tend to grasp the over-all logical structure, to reproduce readily the relation between the major and minor premise, and to formulate promptly the resultant question.

The basic group of subjects displayed a quite different pattern of behavior. These subjects did not, as a rule, immediately perceive the logical relation between the parts of the syllogism. For them, each of the three separate phrases constituted an isolated judgment. Therefore, these subjects repeated separate sentences, reproducing them as if they were unrelated, separate judgments, frequently simplifying them and modifying their form. The communality of the major and minor premises was not explicitly perceived, and the sentences lost virtually all their syllogistic character.

The following syllogism was presented: *Precious metals do not rust. Gold is a precious metal. Does it rust or not?* The following are examples of how this syllogism was repeated (the numbers in parentheses represent the numbers of times the syllogism had been presented).

Subject: Kurb., age eighteen, peasant from remote region, illiterate.

"Do precious metals rust or not? Does gold rust or not?" (1)

Subject: Gal., peasant from remote region, almost illiterate.

"Precious money rusts . . . there was something else, I forget." (1)

"Do precious metals rust or not?" (2)

Subject: Sult., age twenty, peasant from remote region, almost illiterate.

"Precious metals rust." (1)

"Do precious metals rust or not?" (2)

Subject: Iganberdy, age thirty-four, Kirghiz, illiterate.

"Precious metal rusts. Precious gold rusts." (1)

"Does precious gold rust or not?" (2)

"Do precious metals rust or not? Does precious gold rust or not?" (3)

Subject: Mamlak, age thirty-two, peasant, almost illiterate.

"They are all precious . . . gold is also precious . . . does it rust or not?" (1)

The following syllogism was presented: *Rabbits live in large forests. There are no large forests in cities. Are there large cities where there are rabbits?*

Subject: Kul., peasant from remote region, almost illiterate.

"In one city there is a forest. Can there be rabbits there? There is another forest. Can there be rabbits there?" (1)

Subject: Gal., age seventeen, peasant, almost illiterate.

"In one town there is a forest, and there are rabbits. In another large town there is no forest. Can there be rabbits there?" (1)

Subject: Khaidar., age thirty-two, Kirghiz from remote nomad camp, illiterate.

"Here there are large forests . . . are there rabbits in them?" (1)

"Here there are large forests, with rabbits in them. Why are there no rabbits in large cities?" (2)

Subject: Akram., age eighteen, peasant, illiterate.

"There are rabbits in forests. Are there rabbits in large cities or not?" (1)

The following syllogism was presented: *White bears exist only where it is very cold and there is snow. Silk cocoons exist only where it is very hot. Are there places that have both white bears and cocoons?*

Subject: Kul., age twenty-six, peasant, almost illiterate.

"There is a country where there are white bears and white snow. Can there be such a thing? Can white silk grow there?" (1)

"Where there is white snow, white bears live. Where it is hot, there are cocoons. Is this right?" (2)

"Where there is white snow, there are white bears. Where it is hot, there are white silkworms. Can there be such a thing on earth?" (3)

Subject: Rust., age forty-two, peasant, illiterate.

"Where there is white snow, there are white bears, where it is hot, are there cocoons or not?" (1)

"Where it is cold, there are white bears. Where it is hot are there cocoons? Are there such places on earth?" (2)

"Where it is cold, do white bears live? Where it is hot, are there cocoons? Are there such countries on earth?" (3)

The following syllogism was presented: *Books are made of paper. In Japan, paper is made of silk. What are books made of there?*

Subject: Gal., age seventeen, peasant, illiterate.

"In Japan, what are books made of? What are these books made of?" (1)

"What are books everywhere made of? No, if I say different words, it doesn't work." (2)

Subject: Abdur., age thirty, peasant from Yardan village, illiterate.

"All paper is of silk. In Japan paper is of silk." (1)

"All books are made of paper . . . In Japan books are made of silk. Why?"

These examples show that syllogisms are not perceived by these subjects as unified logical systems. The subjects repeat different parts of the syllogisms as isolated, logically unrelated phrases. With some, the subjects grasp the interrogative form of the last sentence, which they then transfer to the formulation of both premises, which they have registered as two isolated questions. In other instances the question formulated in the syllogism is repeated regardless of the preceding premises; thus, the question is perceived as unrelated to the two interconnected premises. In all instances, when a subject repeated the premises he did not give them the character of universal assertions. Rather he converted each into a specific assertion logically unrelated to the other and unusable for drawing the appropriate logical conclusions.

We can thus conclude that syllogisms are not necessarily perceived as a series of propositions of varying degrees of generality that comprise a unified logical structure. They can be perceived as a series of isolated, concrete, and logically unrelated judgments that yield no particular inference and are thus not a means of deduction.

In the course of the experiment it became clear that further study of logical operations required preliminary work on syllogistic figures with the subjects—specifically, work that would stress the universal nature of the premises and their logical interrelations, and that would focus the subjects' attention on these relations.

Subjects with some schooling repeated the syllogisms with no special difficulties. After one or two repetitions, they usually reproduced the syllogistic figures correctly.

## The Process of Deduction

We presented the subjects with two types of syllogisms. One kind contained premises familiar to the subjects from their own practical experience, except that the experience was transferred to new conditions. For example: *Cotton grows well where it is hot and dry. England is cold and damp. Can cotton grow there or not?*

The second sort of syllogism included material unfamiliar to the subjects, and their inferences had to be purely theoretical. For example: *In the Far North, where there is snow, all bears are white. Novaya Zemlya is in the Far North. What color are bears there?*

Subjects living under the most backward conditions (primarily ichkari women) refused to make any inferences even from syllogisms of the first type. They usually declared that they had never been in such unfamiliar places and didn't know whether cotton grew there. Only when the experiment was extended in time and they were requested to answer ("What do my words suggest?") did they agree to draw a conclusion ("From your words, it should be that cotton can't grow there, if it is cold and damp; when it is cold and damp, cotton doesn't grow.").

They refused even more decisively to draw inferences from the second type of syllogism. As a rule, many refused to accept the major premise, declaring that they "had never been in the North and had never seen bears; to answer the question you would have to ask people who had been there and seen them." Frequently they completely ignored the premise and replaced the inferential process by considerations of their own, for example, "There are different kinds of bears; if one was born red, he will stay that way"; or "The world is large, I don't know what kinds of bears there are," and they would introduce general, rumor-based opinions about bears. In short, in each case they would avoid solving the task.

Some subjects completely denied the possibility of drawing any conclusions from syllogisms of this type, declaring that they "could only judge what they had seen," or "didn't want to lie," or that "the question could only be answered by people who had seen them or who knew." Even leading questions ("What do my words suggest?") drew little response. The subjects refused to resort to logical inference from the given premises.

The most typical responses of the subjects, therefore, were a complete denial of the possibility of drawing conclusions from propositions about things they had no personal experience of, and suspicion about any logical operation of a purely theoretical nature, although there was the recognition of the possibility of drawing conclusions from one's own practical experience. Here are some examples in support of these generalizations.

Subject: Abdurakhm., age thirty-seven, from remote Kashgar village, illiterate.

> **Cotton can grow only where it is hot and dry. In England it is cold and damp. Can cotton grow there?**
>
> "I don't know."
>
> **Think about it.**
>
> "I've only been in the Kashgar country; I don't know beyond that . . ."
>
> *Refusal; reference to lack of personal experience.*
>
> **But on the basis of what I said to you, can cotton grow there?**
>
> "If the land is good, cotton will grow there, but if it is damp and poor, it won't grow. If it's like the Kashgar country, it will grow there too. If the soil is loose, it can grow there too, of course."
>
> *Both premises ignored, reasoning conducted within the framework of conditions advanced independently.*
>
> **The syllogism is repeated. What can you conclude from my words?**
>
> "If it's cold there, it won't grow; if the soil is loose and good, it will."
>
> *Conditions of syllogism ignored.*
>
> **But what do my words suggest?**
>
> "Well, we Moslems, we Kashgars, we're ignorant people; we've never been anywhere, so we don't know if it's hot or cold there."
>
> *The same.*
>
> The following syllogism is presented: **In the Far North, where there is snow, all bears are white. Novaya Zemlya is in the Far North and there is always snow there. What color are the bears there?**
>
> "There are different sorts of bears."

*Failure to infer from syllogism.*

The syllogism is repeated.

"I don't know; I've seen a black bear, I've never seen any others . . . Each locality has its own animals: if it's white, they will be white; if it's yellow, they will be yellow."

*Appeals only to personal, graphic experience.*

**But what kind of bears are there in Novaya Zemlya?**

"We always speak only of what we see; we don't talk about what we haven't seen."

*The same.*

**But what do my words imply?** The syllogism is repeated.

"Well, it's like this: our tsar isn't like yours, and yours isn't like ours. Your words can be answered only by someone who was there, and if a person wasn't there he can't say anything on the basis of your words."

*The same.*

**But on the basis of my words—in the North, where there is always snow, the bears are white, can you gather what kind of bears there are in Novaya Zemlya?**

"If a man was sixty or eighty and had seen a white bear and had told about it, he could be believed, but I've never seen one and hence I can't say. That's my last word. Those who saw can tell, and those who didn't see can't say anything!" (At this point a young Uzbek volunteered, "From your words it means that bears there are white.")

**Well, which of you is right?**

"What the cock knows how to do, he does. What I know, I say, and nothing beyond that!"

Subject: Rustam, age forty-seven, peasant from the village of Palman, illiterate.

The cotton syllogism is presented. **Does cotton grow in chilly places?**

"No, you see the climate has got worse here and the cotton has got worse."

**And if it rained all the time, would cotton grow or not?**

"No, cotton doesn't like rain. It was because of the rain that we had no harvest."

**Now, in England it is cold and it rains all the time. Can cotton grow there?**

"I don't know. I've heard of England, but I don't know if cotton grows there."

**It's cold and there's a lot of rain there. Can cotton grow there?**

"If it's cold and there's a lot of rain, only the irrigated kind can grow there, but still there will be no harvest."

*Failure to infer beyond personal experience.*

**And are people involved in cotton-raising there?**

"How should I know?! If it can be sown, people probably raise it."

*Reasoning within the framework of the premises and full-fledged practical inference.*

The white-bears syllogism is presented. **What color are the bears in the North?**

"If there was someone who had a great deal of experience and had been everywhere, he would do well to answer the question."

*Inference not drawn from premise.*

**But can you answer the question on the basis of my words?**

"A person who had traveled a lot and been in cold countries and seen everything could answer; he would know what color the bears were."

*Failure to infer from premises of syllogism and appeal to need for personal experience in order to answer question.*

**Now, in the North, in Siberia, there is always snow. I told you that where there is snow the bears are white. What kind of bears are there in the North in Siberia?**

"I never traveled through Siberia. Tadzhibai-aka who died last year was there. He said that there were white bears there, but he didn't say what kind."

*The same.*


We could scarcely find a better example of how the theoretical operation of inference from syllogisms is dealt with than the responses of this subject, who had only just arrived from the remoter regions of the Kashgar country. The subject refused to discuss any topics that went beyond his personal experience, insisting that "one could speak only of what one had seen," and failing to accept the premises presented to him. Other subjects in the group yielded similar data.

Subject: Khamrak., age forty, miller from remote village, illiterate.

The cotton syllogism is presented. **Can cotton grow where it is cold and damp?**

"No, if the soil is damp and chilly, it can't."

**Now, in England it is damp and chilly. Will cotton grow there?**

Subject's wife volunteers, "It's chilly here too."

**But there it is always cold and damp. Will cotton grow?**

"Me, I don't . . . I don't know what the weather is like there!"

*Data of minor premise are ignored; resorts to personal experience.*

**Cotton can't grow where it is cold, and it's cold in England. Does cotton grow there or not?**

"I don't know . . . if it's cold, it won't grow, while if it's hot, it will. From your words, I would have to say that cotton shouldn't grow there. But I would have to know what spring is like there, what kind of nights they have."

*Possibility of inferring from "your words," but reference to lack of personal experience.*

The white-bears syllogism is presented. **What color are the bears in the North?**

"I don't know what color the bears there are, I never saw them."

*Refusal to draw conclusion because of lack of personal experience.*

**But what do you think?**

"Once I saw a bear in a museum, but that's all."

**But on the basis of what I said, what color do you think the bears there are?**

"Either one-colored or two-colored . . . [ponders for a long time]. To judge from the place, they should be white. You say that there is a lot of snow there, but we have never been there!"

*Attempt to draw conclusion from the words of the interviewer, but again reference to lack of personal experience.*

Subject: Irgash, age thirty, former farmhand, peasant from village of Yardan, illiterate.

The cotton syllogism is presented. **Does cotton grow in England?**

"I don't know if there's cotton there or not."

**But, from my words, what do you think?**

"If it's chilly, if there is snow, then there won't be any there, of course."

*Inference made from interviewer's words.*

The white-bears syllogism is presented. **What kind of bears are there in the North?**

"You've seen them, you know. I haven't seen them, so how could I say?!"

*Refusal to draw conclusion without graphic experience.*

**But on the basis of what I said, what do you think?** The syllogism is repeated.

"But I never saw them, so how could I say?!"

*The same.*

Subject: Nazir-Said, age twenty-seven, peasant from village of Shakhimardan, illiterate.

The following syllogism is presented: **There are no camels in Germany. The city of B. is in Germany. Are there camels there or not?**

Subject repeats syllogism exactly.

**So, are there camels in Germany?**

"I don't know, I've never seen German villages."

*Refusal to infer.*

The syllogism is repeated.

"Probably there are camels there."

**Repeat what I said.**

"There are no camels in Germany, are there camels in B. or not? So probably there are. If it's a large city, there should be camels there."

*Syllogism breaks down, inference drawn apart from its conditions.*

**But what do my words suggest?**

"Probably there are. Since there are large cities, there should be camels."

*Again a conclusion apart from the syllogism.*

**But if there aren't any in all of Germany?**

"If it's a large city, there will be Kazakhs or Kirghiz there."

**But I'm saying that there are no camels in Germany, and this city is in Germany.**

"If this village is in a large city, there is probably no room for camels."

*Inference made apart from syllogism.*

The white-bears and cocoons syllogism is presented.

After being presented several times, the syllogism is repeated accurately.

**What do you think, are there places where there are both white bears and cocoons?**

"There must be. There are large villages in the world. In one collective farm there might be white bears, and in another there might be cocoons."

*Conditions of syllogism accepted; attempts to find solution in imagined graphic situation.*

**And could it happen that white bears steal cocoons?**

"If something tries to injure the cocoons, the peasants will take action. But you're asking if there are such places. I say that there might be."

*Inference apart from conditions of syllogism.*

**But white bears are found only in cold countries, and cocoons only in hot ones.**

"Well, let's say you have a large city with mountains next to it, like here in Shakhimardan. Here you can raise cocoons, and in the mountains there could be bears."

*All subsequent reasoning on the level of imagined compromise situation.*

**But, listen, cocoons can't live where it's cold, and white bears aren't found where it's hot.**

"Once you have bears, it means that they could steal cocoons."

*Graphic image of "thieving bear" dominates.*

Subject: Gasur Akbar, age twenty-six, has lived two years on collective farm, barely literate.

The cotton syllogism is presented. **What do you think, does cotton grow in England?**

"No, if it is humid and chilly, it won't grow."

The white-bears syllogism is presented.

"You say that it's cold there and there's snow, so the bears there are white."

The white-bears and cocoons syllogism is presented.

"No, silkworms live in the spring, and when it's chilly they don't live. Hence there is no country in which there are both white bears and silkworms; it would be cold and the silkworms wouldn't live there."

Subject: Ishankul, age sixty-three, collective farmworker, illiterate, one of the most respected people in the village.

> The cotton syllogism is presented. **So do you think that cotton grows in England?**
>
> "That depends on the climate. If it rains a lot and it's cold, it will turn yellow and not grow."
>
> The white-bears syllogism is presented. **What kind of bears are there in city A in the North?**
>
> "If you say that they are white from the cold, they should be white there too. Probably they are even whiter than in Russia."

Subject: Abdull., age forty-five, chairman of collective farm, barely literate.

> The cotton syllogism is presented. **Well, is there cotton in England?**
>
> "We don't know that; we know that it grows in our country. Now, cotton grows in Tadzhikistan, and people talk and think about it."
>
> The syllogism is repeated. **So does cotton grow in England?**
>
> "It must be that cotton doesn't grow there, wheat grows there. Wheat grows where it's rainy."
>
> The white-bears syllogism is presented. **So what kind of bears are there in city A in the North?**
>
> "If it's very windy and cold there, the bears are of different colors."
>
> **But what do my words suggest?** The syllogism is repeated.
>
> "To go by your words, they should all be white."

For the nonliterate subjects, the processes of reasoning and deduction associated with immediate practical experience follow well-known rules. These subjects can make excellent judgments about facts of direct concern to them and can draw all the implied conclusions, displaying no deviation from the "rules" and revealing much worldly intelligence. The picture changes, however, just as soon as they have to change to a system of theoretical thinking—in this instance, making syllogistic inferences. Three factors substantially limit their capabilities for theoretical, verbal-logical thinking. The first is a mistrust of an initial premise that does not reproduce personal experience. There is also a refusal to accept and use the premise as a point of departure for subsequent reasoning. Frequently the subjects ignored the premise altogether. In continuing to reason only from immediate experience, they did not wish to make judgments outside of this experience, referring to the fact that they "hadn't been there," or that they "hadn't seen" the situations in question, or that they could only say "if they had seen" or "if they knew." They supplanted verbal, logical reasoning with a process of recollection about graphically obtained impressions.

The second factor was the unacceptability of the premises as universal. Rather they were treated as particular messages reproducing some particular phenomenon. Premises deprived of universality yield, naturally enough, only particular information creating no firm logical system or basis for logical inference. Even when the subjects could remember the premise, therefore, they continued to make independent guesses or resort to personal experience.

The third factor, a consequence of the second, involves ready disintegration of the syllogisms into three independent and isolated particular propositions with no unified logic and thus no access for thought to be channeled within this system. The subjects had nothing to do but to try answering the question by sheer guesswork or by recourse to immediate concrete experience. While refusing to use the syllogism for logical inference, our subjects could still use the logical relations fairly objectively if they could rely on their own experience. They refused, however, to use the logical relations when the discursive operations were divorced from immediate experience.

Our remarks, however, refer only to those subjects whose cognitive activity was formed by experience and not by systematic instruction or more complex forms of communication. Other subjects yielded a different picture. They could accept the syllogism's initial premise as the basis for further reasoning, and could grasp its universality. Judgments first given in an immediately familiar context were gradually transferred to independent areas, thus assuming the familiar features of abstract verbal and logical deduction.

The shaping of the foundations of theoretical thinking, as we observed it, can be regarded as one of the most important processes in the historical shaping of consciousness. The summary data presented in Table 8 make evident the differences between the two groups of subjects in dealing with the two types of syllogisms.

Table 8. Mastery of Operation of Inference from Syllogisms

| Group | Solution | Syllogisms associated with experience | | Syllogisms not associated with experience | |
|---|---|---|---|---|---|
| | | Unsolved | Solved | Unsolved | Solved |
| Illiterate peasants from remote villages (15 subjects) | Immediate solution | 6 (40%) | 9 (60%) | 13 (85%) | 2 (15%) |
| | After conditional assumption ("from your words I can gather that . . .") | — | 6 (40%) | 8 (60%) | 4 (30%) |
| Young people with short-term education, farm activists (15 subjects) | Immediate solution | 0 | 15(100%) | 0 | 15(100%) |

# 5

## Reasoning and
## Problem-Solving

What is the structure of reasoning processes at the stage of historical development we are concerned with? How do our subjects combine the operations of logical inference, interrelation of premises, and deduction? What is the relationship between practical experience and verbal, logical reasoning?

In many respects problem-solving forms a model of complex intellectual processes. Every familiar school problem constitutes a complex psychological structure in which the final goal (formulated as the problem's question) is determined by specific conditions. Only by analyzing these conditions can the student establish the necessary relations between the components of the structure in question; he isolates the essential ones and disregards the inessential ones. By getting a preliminary fix on the problem's conditions, the student formulates a general strategy for its solution; in other words, he creates a general logical scheme that determines the direction for further search. This scheme in turn determines the reasoning tactics and the choice of operations that can lead to the making of a decision. Once this is done, the student moves on to the last stage, merging the results with the specified conditions. If the results are in agreement, he is finished; if any of the conditions remains unmet and the results disagree with the initial conditions, the search for the necessary solution continues (Luria and Tsvetkova, 1966).

Any problem-solving process takes its point of departure from its solubility within the framework of a single, closed logical system. In other words, the problem solver cannot go beyond the system of logical relations bounded by the data formulated in the conditions of the problem. He can supply no additional arguments, accessory considerations, or collateral associations from earlier experience. Thus, it would be surprising, to say the least, if a problem-solver who had been asked how much tea there was in two boxes each of a certain weight were to begin to discuss grades of tea, or the place where the tea is stored, or whether it becomes drier under storage. Because of this basic rule, the problem-solving process must be confined by formal conditions, and additional considerations for the subjects cannot be involved. It should make no difference to the problem-solver whether the conditions formulated in the problem correspond to real ones or not.

The facts cited in earlier chapters prompted us to assume that the processes would be different among the uneducated subjects in this study. As yet we did not know to what extent the subjects in our basic group could master operations involving the establishment of relations between individual problem components, or how they performed calculations necessary for obtaining a correct solution. We had, however, every reason to assume that the basic rule of problem-solving (retention of its formal nature, the closed nature of logical systems, and the independence of content from actual conditions) would cause pronounced difficulties among our subjects, whose logical reasoning had been shaped by direct practical experience and whose theoretical thinking was as yet inadequately differentiated from practical thinking.

Only through school instruction and the concomitant creation of special "theoretical" activity could the situation change markedly and the process of problem-solving become an independent discursive activity, assuming forms similar to the familiar forms of verbal and logical and discursive thought that we see in schoolchildren.

The first question that concerned us was how the basic processes needed for problem-solving (analysis of the problem's requirements, generation of hypotheses, determination of solution strategies, and merging of results with initial conditions) are manifested. Second, we wanted to learn the extent to which problem-solving processes depend on the specific content or, more precisely, on the degree to which the conditions of the problem conform to or differ from graphic practical experience. The following two issues determined the basic approach of our analysis.

The subjects were asked to solve a simple problem that was fairly concrete in content and numerical make-up. Examples of such problems are: It is five kilometers from *A* to *B*, and three kilometers from *B* to *C*; how many kilometers is it from *A* to *C*? It takes three hours to go from *A* to *B*, and two hours to go from *B* to *C*; how long does it take to go from *A* to *C*? A man takes three hours to walk from *A* to *B*, while a man on a bicycle does it three times faster; how long will it take the cyclist to go from *A* to *B*? These problems (in which the points of departure and destinations were given the names of villages well-known to the subjects) did not go beyond simple practical problems and required no special school instruction.

Do the subjects accept the problem's conditions and use them as a point of departure in solving the problem, or do they resort to experience or the specific conditions necessary for executing a particular, practical task? To put it differently, does a system of theoretical operations stipulated by the condition of the problem appear, or is this structure replaced by the subjects' practical activity having nothing in common with theoretical analysis and the solution of the problem in question? Naturally, to answer these questions we did not limit ourselves to recording the subjects' answers, but incorporated their solutions into a clinical conversation in which the interviewer, by further questioning, could ascertain the qualitative features of the mental processes involved. When difficulties arose we made the problem more specific and its conditions more graphic.

We conducted two versions of the experiment so that we could better gauge how the system given by the conditions of the problem and the system of the subjects' practical experience were involved in the discursive process. In one version, we gave the subjects problems whose contents corresponded exactly to their practical experience (for example, the distances between the points in question were the same as in reality). Such problems could be solved either by formal logical operations or by appeal to direct experience. In the second version, the contents contradicted the subjects' experience (for example, the distances between points were deliberately changed). The ability to solve such problems would indicate a capacity to disengage oneself from immediate experience, to perceive the problem as a closed, hypothetical system, and to arrive at the solution with a system of formal operations using a provisional assumption as a starting point, even if it contradicted direct practical experience.

To determine whether difficulties in solution were associated with mastery of the particular semantic structure or with the computations, we made an additional study of the solution of simple examples presented apart from the condition of the problem (for example, $30 \div 3 = ?$).

Sixteen illiterate peasants from remote regions took part. As in the earlier series, the comparison group was provided by subjects who had at least short-term school instruction and had been exposed to at least the rudiments of intellectual theoretical operations.

## REASONING IN THE PROBLEM-SOLVING PROCESS

First let us consider the process of solving ordinary problems whose conditions were consistent with practical experience (simple problems).

### Solution of Simple Problems

Subjects who lived in remote villages and had not been influenced by school instruction were incapable of solving even the simplest problems. The reason did not involve difficulties in direct computation (the subjects handled these fairly easily, using special procedures to make them more specific). The basic difficulty lay in abstracting the conditions of the problem from extraneous practical experience, in reasoning within the limits of a closed logical system, and in deriving the appropriate answer from a system of reasoning determined by the logic of the problem rather than graphic practical experience.

As a rule, these subjects refused to perform the required formal logical operations, referring to their lack of personal experience, and resorted directly to guesses that did not stem from the conditions of the problem. Sometimes they introduced additional practical considerations.

Subject: Illi-Khodzh., age twenty-four, woman from remote village, illiterate.

> The following problem is given: **It takes thirty minutes to walk to village X, and it is five times faster on a bicycle. How long will it take on a bicycle?**
>
> "My brother in Dzhizak has a bicycle, and he goes much faster than a horse or a person."
>
> The problem is repeated.
>
> "Five times faster . . . If you go on foot, you will get there in thirty minutes, but if you go by bicycle, you will get there much faster, of course, probably in one or two minutes."
>
> *All reasoning outside of the conditions of the problem.*

The subject declined to deal with the problem further; we can readily see that the resulting difficulties were independent of the computations themselves and the subject's ability to solve the division problem (30 ÷ 5) when it was made specific, for example, when she was asked to divide thirty cookies among five men.

Subject: Nurmat., age thirty-six, woman from village of Yardan, almost illiterate.

> The following problem was given: **It takes twenty hours to go on foot to Dzhizak, or five times faster on a bicycle. How long will it take on a bicycle?**
>
> "Twenty hours on foot to Dzhizak, and five times faster on a bicycle . . . I can't reckon at all. Ten hours, maybe? I know that bicycles go faster than bullock carts. Probably it would get there in about ten hours."
>
> *Failure to begin operations within the given conditions.*
>
> **How do you know?**
>
> "I guessed by myself."
>
> To make the problem more specific, the subject is given twenty buttons.
>
> "If it's twenty hours on foot, you may not get there in ten hours on a bicycle. [Sorts through the buttons, but doesn't use them as a means for

solving the problem.] Probably much faster . . . I don't know, I never rode."

*The proffered assistance is not used and the subject does not go beyond guesswork.*

As a check, the subject was asked to divide thirty rubles among six people. She set out six piles of four buttons each, then added one button to each and said, "If I take half a ruble from each, it still won't be enough . . . Can you divide a ruble? Or do you leave the ones left over?" A simple division operation using external assistance is within the subject's capabilities, but she tries to change to customary practical operations.

Subject: Mukhamed, age twenty, peasant from village of Karasu, slightly literate.

The following problem is given: **It takes thirty minutes to go on foot to a certain village, or five times faster by bicycle. How long will it take on a bicycle?**

Subject answers immediately: "One minute!"

*Guesswork instead of a solution.*

**How did you know?**

"If he goes fast, he will get there in one minute. You said, a man goes on foot to your village. How long will a bicycle take?"

*Problem breaks down upon repetition of the conditions.*

The problem is repeated (the subject repeats the conditions correctly).

"In about one minute, perhaps a little more, perhaps a little less."

*Again guesswork.*

**If a man takes thirty minutes and a bicycle goes five times faster, how will it get there in one minute?**

"I myself haven't seen how they go, but I imagine that they could get there in one minute."

*Again guesswork, with an arbitrary change in the condition.*

**Well, you figure it out.**

"Well, by my reckoning, it would be like this: perhaps a minute, perhaps a half a minute."

*Reference to lack of practical experience.*

The subject is given thirty buttons and asked to use them to solve the problem. The condition is repeated.

"But what village? Karasu? No, it can't be figured out like this. I'll say roughly: perhaps two minutes, perhaps two and a half, or perhaps one, there's nothing to figure here."

*Attempts to make the conditions more specific do not lead to the necessary results; discursive solution again replaced by guesswork.*

It is explained to the subject that "five times faster" means that a bicycle could make the trip five times in the time it took for a man on foot to do it once. **So how much time would it take for one trip?**

"But why should he make five extra trips and waste time like that?!"

*Explanation is grasped in terms of "extra trips."*

**But still, how long would he take to get there?**

"If you were to tell me how many versts it is to the village, I could answer you!"

*Attempts to make the problem more specific.*

**No, think about it. The cyclist spends five times less time.**

"Perhaps while the one on foot was traveling for five or six minutes, the cyclist would cover the distance in a minute!"

*Again guesswork instead of a solution.*

**How long would it take him to go the entire distance?**

"If a man on foot travels for eleven or twelve hours, a cyclist would go five or six times the distance in the same time."

*The same, with new arbitrary conditions.*

**How much time would it take him to get to the village?**

"We don't reckon in hours; I had better reckon in days."

*Appeal to more graphic measures.*

**Well, then, assume that it takes thirty days on foot, and five times faster by bicycle.**

"You'll get there five or six days earlier on a bicycle. The cyclist will have gotten there when the man on foot has been going for five or six days."

*Problem remains unsolved despite more specific conditions.*

**Why do you think it will be five or six, rather than three or four?**

"We Uzbeks usually say five or six, so that's why I said . . ."

*This subject could readily solve a control problem of dividing thirty rubles among five people, by arranging the thirty buttons into five piles.*

Here the basic difficulty is that the subjects refuse to create closed systems using the logical conditions of the problems and to exercise their reasoning within the framework of these conditions. This difficulty forces them to replace the requisite "theoretical" reasoning by direct guesswork. We obtained similar data from other subjects in this group.

Subject: Rustam., age thirty-four, water distributor in the village of Palman, illiterate.

The following question is given: **How long does it take to go from Muyan to Ak-Mazar?** After the answers "one hour" and "thirty minutes" are given, the following problem is given: **It takes thirty minutes to go on foot to Ak-Mazar, or six times faster on a bicycle. How long will a cyclist take?**

"From here to Ak-Mazar on foot . . . on a bicycle . . . probably six or seven minutes."

*Failure to solve the problem.*

**And if you figure it exactly?**

"I couldn't say exactly, only approximately; I myself never went! People who did could tell you . . . so I'm telling you approximately."

*References to lack of personal experience.*

**But I want you to figure it out exactly.** The condition of the problem is repeated; the subject thinks it over and sighs.

"There and back on foot, or only one way? And both ways on a bicycle, or only one?"

**Only one.**

"Well, this is what I think: a man rode there, and another left on foot. The cyclist could go six times, and the last time he would arrive together with the one on foot! Probably it would be six minutes!"

*Attempts to make the solution more specific, then guesswork.*

**Why do you think six minutes?**

"It's easy to get there."

*Motivation by concrete conditions.*

**Now, another man went ten times faster. How soon did he get there?**

"If he went faster . . . Probably he got there in five minutes . . ."

*Again guesswork.*

**But figure it out more precisely!**

"What is there to figure out? If another man could go even faster than the first, then he would also get there sooner."

*Arbitrary change of conditions.*

**No, this one takes exactly the same time. Thirty minutes.**

"You've given me a very difficult problem . . . I can't reckon in minutes."

*Failure to solve problem.*

A control problem with familiar concrete units, namely versts, is given: **It is sixty versts to Namangan, and three times less to Fergana. How many versts is it to Fergana?**

"Twenty versts . . . If it's three times less, it must be twenty!"

*Concrete problem is readily solved.*

As in the preceding cases, numerical operations with familiar concrete entities are performed without difficulty; on the other hand, the inclusion of conditions that operate with abstract categories creates major barriers for logical operations. The subjects replace operations within a closed logical system by reasoning and guesswork that goes beyond the framework of the system; or they attempt to refine the content in ways that are meaningless for carrying out the formal operations necessary for solving the problems. We observe a similar state of affairs in the following examples.

Subject: Faizull., age thirty-five, peasant from village of Palman, illiterate.

The following problem is given: **It takes five minutes to walk to that tree, while a bicycle goes five times faster. How many minutes will it take the cyclist to get to the tree?**

"If he knows how to ride well, he'll get there in two minutes. Perhaps I wouldn't get there in five, but the bicycle would make it in two minutes."

*Appeal to graphic experience and guesswork instead of a solution.*

**No, you have to calculate it exactly.**

"A minute and a half, I think."

*The same.*

The conditions of the problem are repeated.

"I don't know . . . of course, if he rides, he'll get there five times earlier than us. Probably in two and a half minutes."

*The same.*

Another problem is given: **It takes three hours to get to Fergana by bullock cart, or three times faster by train. How long will the train take to get there?**

"An hour."

**How did you know?**

"I once went to Fergana, I was carrying rice, and I raced the horses but didn't overtake the train . . . Some of them go fast."

*Solution by guesswork and appeal to personal experience.*

**Yes, but figure it out exactly.** The problem is repeated.

"If you reckon on average, the train will get to Fergana three times while a cart does it once."

*Attempt to make the conditions more specific.*

**How long will it take the train to get there?**

"Half an hour or three-quarters; an hour if it's a freight train."

*Again guesswork and appeal to concrete experience.*

Our transcripts thus provide unambiguous evidence that the simple computational operations used in everyday practical affairs presented no special difficulties, although these calculations were carried out by wholly concrete procedures. The difficulties that arose always involved a failure to find the solution within the framework of the formal condition of the problem, that is, a failure to perform a discursive operation. The conditions of the problem do not form a closed logical system within which the appropriate computational processes should be carried out. Instead, the subjects either make attempts to answer the question by guesswork or appeal to concrete personal experience by replacing the discursive logical solution with an analysis of the specific conditions of their own practical experience. When the subject transfers the problem onto a different concrete level, he eliminates the difficulties and readily solves the problem.

## Solution of Hypothetical (Conflict) Problems

When the conditions of the problem contradicted actual practical experience, the solution most often completely exceeded the capacities of our basic group of subjects. Upon hearing a condition that deviated from or contradicted their actual experience, the subjects usually refused flatly to try to solve the problem, declaring that the condition was wrong, that "it isn't like that," or that they couldn't solve such a problem. Even asking what it would be like if they were to solve it "on the basis of the interviewer's words" (a procedure that had sometimes succeeded in our earlier experiments) did not improve the situation, and the subjects continued to refuse.

This effect was particularly conspicuous among the subjects who had experienced difficulty with problems whose content did not contradict immediate experience. It was even more pronounced among the following group of subjects, who were able to handle simple problems but not "conditional" ones.

Subject: Khashim., age sixty-seven, watchman for village cooperative, illiterate.

> The interviewer gave the following problem: **It is twenty versts from here to Uch-Kurgan, while Shakhimardan is four times closer.** [In actuality, the reverse is true.] **How many versts is it to Shakhimardan?**
>
> "What! Shakhimardan four times closer?! But it's farther away."
>
> **Yes, we know. But I gave out this problem as an exercise.**
>
> "I've never studied, so I can't solve a problem like that! I don't understand it! Divide by four? No . . . I can't."
>
> *At first, refusal to solve the problem.*
>
> **The problem is repeated.**
>
> "If you divide by four, it'll be . . . five versts . . . if you divide twenty by four, you have five!"
>
> *Subject performs computation and arrives at correct solution.*
>
> **According to the problem, what will it be?**
>
> "Then Shakhimardan will be closer."
>
> The same problem is given with the complication that versts (concrete entities) are converted into abstract time: **How much time will be needed, then, to get to Shakhimardan?**
>
> "People who went there from here said that it was a day's journey on horseback, or two days on foot."
>
> *When conditions are made more complicated, subject again slips back to the level of concrete experience.*

**But according to the problem?**

"I don't understand! You've changed a day's journey into five versts?! I don't understand!"

*Refusal to accept the condition as a starting point.*

**But how would it turn out according to the problem?**

"Figure out how many versts a horse goes in a day; I've never been there, I don't know."

**According to the problem, about how long would it take to go to Shakhimardan?**

"How should I know how long it would take? If I had gone, I could say, but I wouldn't want to lie to no purpose, you know."

*Reference to lack of personal experience.*

**Well, according to the problem, how far was it to Uch-Kurgan?**

"Twenty versts."

**How much time would it take to get there?**

"No, it's six versts to Uch-Kurgan, but according to you it's twenty . . . I can't understand you any more. This problem calls for someone who has studied in school, I can't solve it."

*Refusal to reason on a conditional level.*

**But if the problem says that it's twenty versts, how long will it take to get there?**

"According to your problem it's twenty versts, but someone who went there said it was six! I don't understand."

*The same.*

**The problem isn't true. I gave it on purpose to check your arithmetic.**

"Well, how long would it take a man to go twenty versts?" (Ponders.)

*New motivation and attempts to figure out the time.*

**How long does it take now to get to Uch-Kurgan?**

"People who go say it's six versts."

**Well, for example, could you prepare a pilaf in the time it takes a man to go there?**

"Well, if you're hungry, you would make it in a hurry, while if you're not you would do it slower and more carefully. If you have four hungry men, one of them will cut up the fat, another the carrots, and it'll all be ready right away!"

*Translation onto concrete level does not provide a means for solving problem. Extraneous conditions make it impossible to obtain a measure.*

**But if, as the problem says, it's twenty versts to Uch-Kurgan, how long would you take?**

"Twenty versts by four . . . if you put it that way . . . five versts in an hour, so twenty versts would take four hours."

*When translated onto a concrete numerical level, subject performs numerical operations.*

This record is typical. The subjects can be made to solve the problem when they operate with concrete entities (versts). But when the problem changes to an abstract level (time), the subjects are incapable of reasoning about conditions divorced from practical experience, and they slip back into arguments based on experience. Only when this experience is specially narrowed can they perform the appropriate calculations. The difficulties involved are even more apparent in the following subject.

Subject: Khamrak., age thirty-six, peasant from remote village, slightly literate.

**From Shakhimardan to Vuadil it is three hours on foot, while to Fergana it is six hours. How much time does it take to go on foot from Vuadil to Fergana?**

"No, it's six hours from Vuadil to Fergana. You're wrong . . . it's far and you wouldn't get there in three hours."

*Computation is readily performed, but condition of problem is not accepted.*

**That makes no difference; a teacher gave this problem as an exercise. If you were a student, how would you solve it?**

"But how do you travel—on foot or on horseback?"

*Slips back to level of concrete experience.*

**It's all the same—well, let's say on foot.**

"No, then you won't get there! It's a long way . . . if you were to leave now, you'd get to Vuadil very, very late in the evening."

*Condition that contradicts experience is not accepted.*

**All right, but try and solve the problem. Even if it's wrong, try to figure it out.**

"No! How can I solve a problem if it isn't so?!"
*Refusal to solve conditional problem.*

The transcripts show how readily problems whose conditions correspond to reality are solved, and how difficult it is for the subjects to accept conditions that do not hold true in their own experience and to perform the associated formal logical operations. Several examples show how sharply the ability to solve problems conforming to practical experience contrasts with the inability to solve problems whose conditions contradict this experience. These data convincingly demonstrate the degree of difficulty in trying to induce our subjects to perform formal logical reasoning independent of content. Here is an instance.

Subject: Khamid., age thirty-seven, worker from Urshek (remote collective farm), illiterate.

> A problem is given whose conditions do not exactly conform to reality:
> **It is four hours on foot to Vuadil, and eleven hours to Fergana. How much more of a trip is it to Fergana?**
>
> "Vuadil is halfway there. It's three hours from here to Vuadil, and another three from Vuadil to Fergana."
> *Change of conditions in conformity with actual experience.*
>
> **But what is it according to the problem?** The conditions of the problem are repeated.
>
> "Three hours farther."
>
> **How did you know?**
>
> "I tell you, Vuadil is halfway, and then the road from Vuadil to Shakhimardan is poor, and beyond that it's good."
> *Justification of solution by concrete conditions.*
>
> **And what was the problem?**
>
> Subject repeats the conditions of the problem correctly.
>
> **How much farther is it to Fergana?**
>
> "Three hours farther!"
>
> **How did you figure it out?**
>
> "It's a bad road from here to Vuadil!"

*The same.*

**But what was said in the problem?**

"You want to know how much farther it is to Fergana than to Vuadil?"

The conditions of the problem are repeated.

"Three hours longer! Look, it's eleven hours from here to Fergana. But if you leave from Fergana, you'll get to Vuadil in four hours, and from there you'll need seven hours, because it's a hard road."

A "conditional" problem that conflicts with actual experience is given: **Suppose it were to take six hours to get from here to Fergana on foot, and a bicycle was twice as slow?**

"Then a bicycle would get there in three hours!"

*Solution on a level corresponding to practical reality.*

**No, a teacher gave this problem as an exercise—suppose that the bicycle were twice as slow.**

"If the cyclist makes good time, he will get to Fergana in two and a half or three hours. According to your problem, though, if the bicycle breaks down on the way, he'll arrive later, of course. If there's a breakdown, he'll be two or three hours late."

*Search for conditions under which the problem would conform to reality.*

The conditions of the problem are repeated.

(Subject ponders.) "Probably he'll get there in eight hours . . . probably if the bicycle breaks down, he'll be two hours late . . ."

*The same.*

**And if the bicycle doesn't break down, but that's simply the way the problem says it is?**

"If it doesn't break down, he'll make it not just in six hours but in three."

*Refusal to solve problem on conditional level unsupported by concrete conditions.*

**But how do you solve this problem? Forget that it isn't true. A teacher gave it to check on his pupil's ability to figure out.**

"He'll get there in eight hours . . . but still, the bicycle probably broke down. The cyclist would also stop in Vuadil before going on; if something broke down, he would stop too. That's why he's late."

*In operating on conditional level, multiplication is replaced by addition; justification again sought in terms of concrete circumstances.*

All these examples indicate the importance of conformity to concrete practical experience. If the problem's conditions conform to reality, they are accepted; if not, even the admission of such conditions becomes impossible, and the subjects continue to operate on a concrete practical level, distorting the problem to conform to actual conditions or ignoring the conditions altogether and working through a concrete problem, rather than a "hypothetical" one, which they solve in terms of practical experience. All this clearly shows that *the formal operation of problem-solving presents major, sometimes insurmountable difficulties for these subjects.* All this becomes comprehensible if we recall that their thought processes operate on the level of graphic and functional practical experience.

As we could anticipate from our previous results, subjects with at least short-term school instruction or wider social relations express themselves differently and begin to give evidence of a capacity to solve conditional problems involving formal logical operations.

Subject: Kadyr., student in village school for several months.

**It takes thirty minutes to go on foot to Mazar, or six times faster by bicycle. How long will it take a cyclist to get to Mazar?**

"Thirty minutes, and six times faster . . . that means one-sixth of thirty minutes, or five minutes."

A "conditional" problem is given: **A cyclist takes forty minutes to get to Mazar, while a man on foot goes eight times faster. How long does it take the man on foot to get to Mazar?**

"Well, now, if you say it's eight times faster, it means the man on foot will take 240 minutes."

*Computations are changed because of confusion of notions of "faster" and "greater."*

**Is that true?** The problem is repeated.

"So it's the other way around?! Then the man on foot takes five minutes! You have to take one-eighth of forty."

*Solution is readily achieved.*

Another "hypothetical" problem that conflicts with reality is given: **Suppose it were to take three hours to go on foot to Fergana, and twelve hours to Vuadil. [In actuality, the reverse is true.] How much faster would a man arrive in Fergana?**

"Then he would get there four times sooner."

This subject clearly demonstrates the capacity to perform hypothetical, theoretical operations independently of his own practical personal experience. It is of considerable interest that this shift and the capacity to perform "theoretical" operations of formal discursive and logical thinking appear after relatively short-term school instruction. The significance of schooling lies not just in the acquisition of new knowledge, but in the creation of new motives and formal modes of discursive verbal and logical thinking divorced from immediate practical experience. Table 9 on the following page gives our results for different groups of subjects.

Table 9. Mastery of the Process of Problem-Solving

| Group | Solution | Simple problems | | Conflict problems | |
|---|---|---|---|---|---|
| | | Unsolved | Solved | Unsolved | Solved |
| Illiterate peasants from remote villages (16 subjects) | Immediate solution | 4 (25%) | 12 (75%) | 13 (81%) | 3 (19%) |
| | After conditions made more specific | 0 | 16 (100%) | 12 (75%) | 4 (25%) |
| Young people with short-term education (7 subjects) | Immediate solution | 0 | 7 (100%) | 0 | 7 (100%) |

# 6

## Imagination

We have cited a considerable amount of data showing how direct, practical experience dominates the consciousness of unschooled subjects, and how much they prefer relationships arising from practical activity to abstract logical operations. We would expect, therefore, that relations resulting from direct, practical experience will determine the framework of their imagination or fantasy, and will make separation from graphic experience difficult.

Modern psychology distinguishes certain levels within imagination, maintaining that "reproductive" imagination differs from creative imagination. Imagination can be firmly linked with practical experience or can occur within a system of verbal, logical thinking. This approach forces us to go beyond vague references to "fantasy" and attempt to view imagination in a more discriminating way, distinguishing between different levels in semantic content and in the structures of the underlying psychological systems.

Child psychology has made the shift from an undifferentiated description of facts about imagination to a more articulated analysis. Psychologists began by assuming that preschool children have a vigorous, unrestrained fantasy life, and ended up by establishing that young children's imagination is bounded by the limits of immediate memory. It has only a "reproductive" nature, and true creative imagination makes its first real appearance at a later developmental stage.

Aside from distinguishing "reproductive" and "creative" imagination, we should also distinguish between the motives leading to their appearance. All the available facts indicate that imagination begins to display the features of a complexly motivated activity only fairly late in development. In the earlier stages, it continues for quite a while to be tied to the immediate situation, thus keeping like all other mental processes a "nonarbitrary" nature.

What are the psychological features of imagination at different stages of social and historical development? As yet we have no reliable means for providing a complete answer to this question, so our facts provide only limited and partial information.

Our task was to study those forms of imagination accessible not only to highly skilled people such as storytellers and *akyns* (folk poets or singers), who have made a specialty of a specific type of imagination, but rather those characterizing any ordinary person whose practical experience was typical in a given historical setting. At the time of our investigations, we did not yet have procedures that yielded models of imaginative activity that could be analyzed objectively or completely. Such models were much more difficult to develop than models for the processes of generalization, deduction, or reasoning. As a result, therefore, we deliberately restricted our investigation of fantasy to analyzing how our subjects freely formulated questions that expressed, to some degree, the extent and nature of their interests, and how they set up imaginary situations based on certain specified assumptions.

## EXPERIMENTS WITH FREE QUESTIONING

Here the aim was to determine to what degree our subject could formulate free questions and to what extent these questions went beyond immediate practical experience. We had every reason to assume that subjects whose practical experience was relatively restricted would either be unable to formulate complicated questions at random or would require special circumstances to do so. In addition, we could assume that both the ability to formulate questions and the content of the questions themselves would vary in accordance with the shifts taking place in the social life and practical experience of our subjects.

We carried out an appropriate series of observations, with a full understanding of the limitations of this oversimplified method and of the restricted nature of the conclusions which could be drawn. The procedure in some ways represented the reverse of the questionnaire approach: the subjects themselves were asked to pose any three questions to the experimenter.

If the subject had difficulty (as frequently happened), an auxiliary situation was suggested; the subjects were told to imagine that they were coming to school and could ask the teacher anything they wanted to know. Sometimes the experiment was transferred to an imaginary third person, and the subjects were asked to say what their neighbors might ask if they came to school or if a city person were to come to their village. The investigator described the course of the subjects' attempts to formulate questions as well as the contents of the questions asked.

Fifty-three subjects took part in this series of experiments: they included illiterate peasants from remote regions (21); slightly literate people who had attended short-term school courses (10); and people with one or two years' schooling and collective-farm activists (22).

As a rule, the illiterate peasants had considerable difficulty. About a third of them refused altogether to pose any questions. They maintained that they didn't know what to ask, or that they knew only their own work ("to be able to ask, you need knowledge, and I don't have it"), and at the end of the conversation they would ask the interviewer himself to furnish questions that they could answer. Even when the task was narrowed down and they were told that the investigators were from Moscow and it was suggested that they ask about life in other cities, they said that they had "never been anywhere," or "how could you ask about cities that you hadn't seen?" Thus they had a limited capacity for actively formulating any questions. While able to answer questions posed by the investigator (sometimes in considerable detail), they were unable to pose them actively themselves.

Subject: Burkhash., Kirghiz from village in region of Uch-Kurgan, illiterate.

**Ask me any three questions. What would you like to know?**

"I don't know how to obtain knowledge . . . where would I find the questions? For questions you need knowledge. You can ask questions when you have understanding, but my head is empty."

*Refusal to ask questions, reference to lack of knowledge.*

**Well, for example, you're drinking tea—do you know how it grows in hot countries?**

"I don't know anything about tea, I take it from the cooperative and drink it."

*The same.*

**Further attempts to obtain questions were unsuccessful.**

Subject: Tadzhib, age thirty, peasant, illiterate.

**Ask me three questions. What interests you?**

"I can't imagine what to ask about—I only know about spadework, nothing else . . . To ask questions you need knowledge, and all we do is hoe weeds in the fields . . . It would be better for you to ask me."

*The same.*

Subject: Irgash, age thirty, peasant from village of Yardan, illiterate.

**Ask me some questions. What interests you?**

"I don't know what to ask."

*Refusal to ask questions.*

**Well, for example, we come from another place, from other cities. Ask me about other cities. What interests you?**

"I like the place where I live best, and other cities don't interest me at all."

**Aren't you interested in what people do there?**

"I haven't seen what people do in other cities, so how can I ask?"

*Refers to lack of experience, rendering questions impossible.*

**Perhaps you're interested in what kind of animals, or people, or buildings they have?**

"But I haven't seen them, so what could I ask?"

*The same.*

It would be incorrect to conclude, on the basis of the transcripts, that these subjects lacked all interests whatsoever. They revealed an active interest in their own direct experiences. What is important is that, within the experimental situation (no matter how natural we tried to make it and how much we prepared the questions by incorporating them into long, casual conversations), the subjects were unable to formulate questions independently, referring to their "lack of necessary knowledge" and remaining within a framework that reproduced their immediate practical experience. Keeping in mind all the stipulations that must be made, we see here pronounced difficulty in disengaging oneself from immediate experience and formulating questions that go beyond it.

Other subjects with similar background confused theoretical questions with practical demands and expressed their immediate wishes and needs, or created an imaginary situation in which questions of knowledge were made to be justifiable in practice.

Subject: Akhmet, age forty-four, Kirghiz from remote mountain camp, illiterate.

> "We aren't interested in anything, we need only harvest with the sickle and chop wood with the ax . . . We ask for many horses and land from the government . . . When they come and ask how many cows we have, we answer, because we know . . . when autumn comes we gather in the harvest, that much we know . . . But we don't know what to ask about."

*Refusal to ask questions and references to lack of knowledge.*

Subject: Kadyr., age sixty-eight, from remote mountain camp, illiterate.

> After unsuccessful attempts to obtain independently formulated questions, the interviewer attempted to define the expected questions more precisely. **What would you like to see—other countries, other cities—and what would you like to learn about them?**

> "Probably there are interesting cities, as you say, but I don't know what's interesting about them. I know that I won't get to see them . . . They took my horse away, and the road is long; I can't even imagine how I would get there."

*Practical question substituted.*

**But if you could see everything, what would you like to find out?**

> (Subject laughs.) "No, I'm already old, why should I learn? I can't talk to no purpose, I have no imagination."

*Refusal to ask questions and reference to lack of imagination.*

Subject: Isamutd., age thirty-four, worker from Mikhnat collective farm, completed literacy program.

**What three questions would you like to ask?**

"Well, if someone comes and asks something about agriculture, they ask how to make our work easier . . . and then they ask how to irrigate . . . those are the questions they'll ask us."

*Creates special condition.*

**But what questions would you like to ask me yourself? What would you like to know, what interests you?**

"Aside from these questions, I'm interested in how to study, how to make my way."

*Independently poses a series of questions about his plans.*

Subject: Akhmetzhan, age thirty-one, collective farmer from village of Shakhimardan, completed literacy program.

**Ask me three questions, any you want, and I'll answer.**

"The main thing I'm interested in is learning; when I become literate and am able to answer well, I'll be able to tell you what interests me . . . The first thing I would ask is, here I am, illiterate, I don't even read newspapers and can't pose questions—and how would you make me literate?"

*Creates imaginary situation about which he could ask if he were literate; confuses questions and wishes.*

**But ask me questions anyway!**

"Well, you just spoke about white bears. I don't understand where they came from (ponders). And then you mentioned America. Is it governed by us or by some other power?"

*Questions concern only information just obtained.*

Thus peasants actively involved in collective farms and who had short-term instruction were able to formulate questions actively, but resorted to the curious procedure of creating an imaginary situation in which the formulation of questions seemed natural or, as in the last instance, formulated questions within the framework of data that had just been communicated to them.

The limited capacities of these illiterate and only barely literate peasants for disengaging themselves from direct experience created major barriers to the active formulation of questions of knowledge. The data obtained from subjects who had undergone short-term systematic instruction and were actively involved in collective-farm life contrast with the above material. These subjects formulated actively questions with no hesitation and with no recourse to imaginary situations for assistance. Their questions also differed markedly, expressing much broader content. They were distinctly questions of knowledge, addressing themselves primarily to pressing problems of social life and related to acquired knowledge or associated stable cognitive interests. Here are some examples.

Subject: Siddakh, age nineteen, studied for two years in a school for adults, works on collective farm.

**Ask me any three questions.**

"Well, what could I do to make our kolkhozniks better people? How can we obtain bigger plants, or plant ones which will grow to be like big trees? And then I'm interested in how the world exists, where things come from, how the rich become rich and why the poor are poor."

*Readily formulates questions of knowledge.*

Subject: Khushv., age twenty-seven, studied for two years in school for adults, works on collective farm.

**Ask me three questions, any you like.**

"I've never been anywhere or seen anything, so how could I have questions?"

*First refuses to formulate questions.*

**But still, ask me whatever you like.**

"Well, we asked the teacher how silk and velvet are produced . . . he didn't answer, but it's something we're interested in."

*Reproduction of question asked in school; then independent formulation of practical questions.*

**And another question.**

"I don't know . . . well, for instance, why is it wrong to slaughter sheep in the spring?"

**And a third.**

"Why cooperatives haven't yet been opened in the village, where they're very much needed!"

Subject: Aziz, age thirty-six, organizer of Mikhnat farm, studied in agronomy program for two and a half months.

**Ask me three questions you would like to have answered.**

Subject responds immediately: "How can life be made better? Why is the life of a worker better than that of a peasant? How can I acquire knowledge more readily? Also: why are city workers more skilled than peasants?"

*Readily formulates questions.*

Subject: Badayab, age thirty, worker on Mikhnat farm, finished literacy program.

**Ask me three questions that interest you.**

"We have heard that industry has increased very much. Why don't we have enough cotton? There are state farms and kolkhozes. Eventually the kolkhozes become state farms. Why does the state farm take our workers—twenty people just went to them recently? And also: they planted Egyptian cotton in the kolkhoz, and got a poor yield, but it grew well for us. Why does that happen?"

*Readily formulates questions stemming from farm practice.*

In the next group, we clearly see the subjects' difficulty in formulating questions independently, combined with their attempts to avoid the difficulty by creating an imaginary situation in which the formulation would become meaningful.

Subject: Illi-Khodzh., age twenty-two, woman from village of Shamardan, slightly literate.

**Ask me three questions, any you want.**

"I'll give you one. Here I am now, but when I go to village X, they ask me, 'You were in Samarkand, what are the buses like there? Do they have hands and feet? How do they move?' I can't explain properly, and I'm very embarrassed . . . and then . . . I don't know what to ask."

*Creates special situation in which she will be asked, and reproduces questions of imaginary interlocutors.*

Our data adequately confirm that the mental life of these subjects changed radically because of collective social labor and at least some systematic education. Table 10 summarizes the data from various groups of subjects.

Table 10. Formulation of Questions

| Group | Refusal to formulate | Formulation of practical questions with the aid of an imaginary situation | Formulation of questions of knowledge |
|---|---|---|---|
| Illiterate peasants from remote villages (21 subjects) | 13 (62%) | 8 (38%) | 0 |
| Peasants who completed literacy program (10 subjects) | 0 | 8 (80%) | 2 (20%) |
| Young people with one or two years' schooling, farm activists (22 subjects) | 0 | 2 (9%) | 20 (91%) |

# 7

## Self-Analysis
## and Self-Awareness

This chapter attempts to determine the extent to which our subjects were able to treat their own inner life in a generalized fashion, to single out particular psychological traits in themselves, to analyze their interior world, and to evaluate their intrinsic qualities. It is to be understood that the data are of a preliminary nature.

Since Descartes, idealistic philosophers and psychologists have maintained that self-awareness is a primary and irreducible property of mental life, with no history in and of itself. The conviction that self-awareness is primary underlay Descartes' maxim, *cogito ergo sum,* and was one source of idealistic psychology.

The initial assumptions of representatives of subjectivist philosophy can vary. Rationalistic philosophers regard as primary and irreducible not only the awareness of one's private world but also those logical categories into which "immediate experience" is molded. Adherents of phenomenalism regard the "immediate data of consciousness" as perceptible sensations, taking them to include not just the irreducible elements of one's inner life but also "elements of the world" understood as subjective states of sentient beings who perceive the world. But rationalists and phenomenologists share one basic assumption, namely that the subjective world is primary while the reflection of the external world is derivative and secondary. This conviction impels the adherents of this view to seek the sources of consciousness and self-awareness in the depths of the human spirit or in the elements of brain structures, while completely disregarding the environment which the human brain reflects. (See Eccles, 1970; Luria, 1967; Gurgenidze and Luria, 1972, for discussion of these issues.)

There is every reason to think that self-awareness is a product of sociohistorical development and that reflection of external natural and social reality arises first; only later, through its mediating influence, do we find self-awareness in its most complex forms. Accordingly, we should approach self-awareness as a product of consciousness of the external world and of other people, and should seek its social roots and traits in the stages through which it is shaped in society.

The notion that self-awareness is a secondary and socially shaped phenomenon was formulated by Marx: "At first, man looked at himself as if in a mirror, except that it is another person. Only by relating to Paul as to one like himself can Peter begin to relate to himself as a person." Despite the fact that the notion of the social origin of self-awareness arose more than a century ago in materialistic philosophy, there have not yet been adequate attempts in psychological research to show that this view is correct or to follow the specific stages through which this phenomenon is shaped socially.

## EXPERIMENTS WITH SELF-ANALYSIS AND SELF-EVALUATION

Our means of objectively studying elementary forms of subjective states (self-sensation, emotional experiences) are unreliable and will be omitted from consideration here. As before, our primary interest lies in the higher and most complex mental activities, in which the shaping influence of social experience can be particularly pronounced. We deliberately narrow down our sphere of interest, therefore, and describe how our subjects were able to relate to their own personality characteristics in a general way, delineate their own character traits, and consciously formulate their psychological peculiarities.

Our initial hypothesis was that processes of perceiving one's own qualities, self-analysis, and self-evaluation are shaped by the conditions of social existence; the formulation of one's own psychological features is a complex process taking shape under the direct influence of the same social practices that determine other aspects of mental life; and that human beings first make judgments of others and perceive others' judgments about themselves, and then, under the influence of these judgments, are able to formulate judgments about themselves. There is virtually no psychological research on this topic. The only exception comes from the field of child psychology, where recently there has been animated discussion about the role of communication between the child and those persons in his environment who shape his self-evaluation.

Some Soviet studies demonstrate that self-evaluation and self-analysis take shape during postnatal development and that nothing could be further from the truth than the notion that direct awareness of one's own mental qualities and capabilities is given at the outset and undergoes no subsequent development.

Our method of research was simple. In the course of a discussion, we would ask the subject how he evaluated his own character, in what way he differed from other people, and what positive traits and shortcomings he could discern in himself. Then we asked similar questions about other people such as relatives, kolkhoz acquaintances, or inhabitants of the same village.

In view of these procedural limitations we analyzed not so much the specific content of the answers or the particular qualities pointed out, but rather the capacity for making one's own mental qualities the subject of analysis and of being aware of them. We were particularly attentive to facts that might indicate that, at certain stages of development, the process of singling out intrinsic mental qualities gives way to pointing out external circumstances, everyday needs, actions, and so forth. We hoped to be able to compare data obtained in conversations with subjects of different groups who have experienced different forms of communication and differing levels of education.

Fifty-two subjects took part in this series, of which twenty were in our first group (illiterate peasants from remote villages), fifteen were active members of collective farms with experience in discussing kolkhoz issues collectively, and seventeen were students in technical schools or people with at least a year or two of formal education. The bulk of the material was gathered by the author, the remainder by V. V. Zakharova.

As our observations showed, the task of analyzing one's own psychological features or subjective qualities went beyond the capabilities of a considerable proportion of our subjects. In general, subjects in the first group failed the task. As a rule, they either refused to name positive or negative qualities in themselves or dealt with the question by describing concrete and material aspects of their lives. Sometimes they pointed to having "bad neighbors" as one of their "shortcomings," or, in other words, they ascribed the undesirable characteristic to other people in their environment. They frequently found it much easier for them to characterize other people than to characterize themselves.

Indications of a developing self-evaluation in this group first show up in the subjects' characterizations of their own qualities on the basis of what other people say. The subjects declared that, "going by what those around them say," they had certain shortcomings, argued with their neighbors, didn't work fast enough, and so forth. Typically, they most frequently replaced a characterization of intrinsic qualities by a description of concrete forms of external behavior. Particularly noticeable here were facts pointing to the decisive role of collective activities in the development of self-awareness; these activities, such as joint planning, discussion of the efficiency of brigade work, evaluation of one's own work efficiency, and so forth, became prominent and assumed the form of deliberate, planned relations in making the change to collective forms of economy. In shaping self-awareness, we can regard the role of collective economy as the one fundamental fact unearthed by our research.

At a certain stage of social development, the analysis of one's own individual peculiarities frequently gave way to an analysis of group behavior, and the individual "I" was frequently replaced by the collective "we," taking the form of an evaluation of the behavior or efficiency of the subject's group (brigade, team, or collective farm as a whole). Frequently one's own qualities (or those of the group) were evaluated by comparing individual (or group) behavior with social norms or demands imposed on the individual or group.

Only in the later developmental stages—primarily among young people actively involved in progressive social life and with at least some education—could we discern a process of singling out and evaluating personal qualities. Here, as well, the analysis remained tied in many ways to the subject's evaluation of how such individual qualities related to the demands of social life.

**Subject: Nurmat., age eighteen, woman from remote village, barely literate.**

After a lengthy conversation about people's characteristics and their individual differences, the following question was asked: **What short-comings are you aware of in yourself, and what would you like to change about yourself?**

"Everything's all right with me. I myself don't have any shortcomings, but if others do, I point them out . . . As for me, I have only one dress and two robes, and those are all my shortcomings."

*"Shortcomings" understood as things that are lacking.*

**No, that's not what I'm asking you about. Tell me what kind of a person you are now and what you would like to be. Aren't there any differences?**

"I would like to be good, but now I'm bad; I have few clothes, so I can't go to other villages like this."

*General formula interpreted in terms of material shortages.*

**And what does "be good" mean?**

"To have more clothes."

**And what shortcomings does your sister have?**

"She's still young, she's small and can't speak well . . . But how could I know, since I'm here and she's in another village . . . My brother, he's learned well, there's nothing he needs to change."

*Refusal to discuss sister's traits if she isn't here.*

**Subject: Murza Shiral., age fifty-five, peasant from village of Yardan, illiterate.**

**Do you think that people are all the same or different?**

"No, they're not the same. There are different ones [holds up fingers]: here's a landowner, here's a farmhand."

**Do you know what the differences are between individuals, say, between your acquaintances?**

"Only they themselves know."

**Well, what are you like? Describe your character.**

"My character is very good-natured. Even if it's a youngster who's before me, I use the polite form of address and speak courteously . . . You have to understand everything, and I don't."

*Description of own behavior.*

**Still, do you have any shortcomings?**

"I have many shortcomings, food, clothing, everything."

**Well, there are other people here in the village; are you the same as them or not?**

"They have their own hearts and different conversations, and they speak different words."

**Well, compare yourself to them and describe your character.**

"I'm a good-natured person, I talk to big people like a big person, to little people like a little person, and to middle-sized people like a middle-sized person . . . That's all I can say, there's nothing else that remains."

*The same.*

Subject: Karambai Khamb., age thirty-six, peasant from village of Yardan, illiterate.

**Well, now, take yourself, Karambai, and your guest here, Ismat. What is the difference between you?**

"There's no difference at all. Once there's a soul it means we're the same."

**What shortcomings and good qualities do you have? What's your character like? You know what character is?**

"Yes!"

**People can be good or bad, hot-tempered or calm. What sort of person are you?**

"What can I say about my own heart?"

**But who could tell about your heart other than you yourself?**

"How can I talk about my character? Ask others; they can tell you about me. I myself can't say anything."

*Reference to the fact that others can judge a man's character.*

**What would you like to change or improve in yourself?**

"I was a farmhand; I have a hard time and many debts, with a measure of wheat costing eighteen rubles—that's what troubles me."

**Well, people are different, and have different characters; what are you like?**

"If I have a lot of money, I buy things and then I'm happy; if I don't have things I'm sad."

*Derives own situation from the circumstances.*

**Well, you have friends here in Yardan. Describe their character.**

"There's Akram, and there's Ismat. They're different, of course. How can you know another's heart? One doesn't talk like the other . . . They're both good-natured . . . except that Akram is quick to get angry, but not Ismat."

*Evaluation of others much more complete.*

Subject: Tyurakil, age thirty-eight, Kirghiz from mountain-pasture camp, illiterate.

**What sort of a person are you, what's your character like, what are your good qualities and shortcomings? How would you describe yourself?**

"I came here from Uch-Kurgan, I was very poor, and now I'm married and have children."

*Question understood in terms of external conditions of life.*

**Are you satisfied with yourself or would you like to be different?**

"It would be good if I had a little more land and could sow more wheat."

**And what are your shortcomings?**

"This year I sowed one pood of wheat . . . We've already gathered the hay and will harvest the wheat, and we're gradually fixing the shortcomings."

*Again everything refers to external conditions of life.*

**Well, people are different—calm, hot-tempered, or sometimes their memory is poor. What do you think about yourself?**

"We behave well—if we were bad people, no one would respect us."

*Self-evaluation in terms of social behavior.*

Subject: Dusmat., age thirty, formerly farmhand in remote village, now quarry-worker, illiterate.

**What good qualities and shortcomings do you see in yourself? Are you satisfied with yourself or not?**

"No, I'm not satisfied . . . You see, I work here, and I might be able to rest here after eight hours' work, but as it is I have to travel three or four versts.''

*Shortcomings related to situation.*

**Tell me everything about your general situation. What shortcomings do you yourself have?**

"Yes . . . well, for instance, my clothing's poor . . . after all, I'm no longer young.''

*The same.*

**I understand. But, in your own mind, are you satisfied or not?**

"No . . . I have no shortcomings, except in learning. I have no time off, because there's no one else to work . . . and then these newcomers don't know how to deal with work, we have to teach them.''

*The same.*

In all these cases, questions probing for an analysis of personal qualities were either not grasped at all or were related to external material circumstances or everyday situations. Attempts to explain that the questions referred to personal traits and that shortcomings should be understood not as material shortages but as intrinsic qualities led to unfortunate results. The conversations continued to revolve around the subjects' external material needs or personal circumstances. Only in very rare instances did we encounter evaluations coming from other sources.

The next, transitional group of subjects usually characterized others much more completely. They resembled the group just described, but in addition to evaluations of qualities manifested in their external behavior, individuals showed a more marked tendency to analyze their own traits in accordance with the evaluations of others, and the appearance of an attempt to evaluate their own traits against norms characteristic of an "ideal me." As a rule, this type of self-evaluation was particularly pronounced for subjects who involved themselves in collective life, took part in kolkhoz meetings, and whose behavior was evaluated by others. The increasing role of social evaluation, under whose influence self-evaluation takes shape, comes to be more and more predominant.

Subject: Illi-Khodzh., age twenty-two, village woman, discarded the veil a month earlier, barely literate, taking literacy courses.

**What are your good and bad qualities?**

"A good thing is that I came out and discarded the veil, while before I used to wear it; I didn't know anything, and now I'm studying."

**Well, what are you dissatisfied with in yourself now? Do you have shortcomings in memory or thinking?**

"I'm very pleased with myself, except that I have headaches and I sweat, so I feel bad in class; they sent me to the doctor, but the medicine doesn't help. Generally everything's fine with me, but in the last class I couldn't quite understand the multiplication problems."

*Points to external shortcomings and learning difficulties.*

**What shortcomings does your husband's sister have?**

"She just died, I can't say anything about her; a while ago she didn't give back two of my blankets, and I didn't say anything."

*Talks about concrete actions.*

Subject: Bayakhok., age thirty, peasant, illiterate.

**Tell me what good and bad traits you see in yourself.**

"I have a big shortcoming: I borrowed 125 rubles and I can't pay them back."

*Refers to material shortages.*

**Can it be that you have no shortcomings, that you wouldn't like to change anything in yourself for the better?**

"I'm a good person, everyone knows me, I'm not rude to anyone, and I always lend a hand. I feel good about myself, there's nothing to change."

**Are you satisfied with your memory and thinking?**

"If someone says a bad word about me, or speaks badly or me, I never forget that word until I give the person a thrashing, so I think that I have a good memory. To be sure, I can't read or write, and that's a shortcoming, of course. If I plan something, I always follow through; what I undertake to do, I always do."

*Evaluates own characteristics on basis of situation.*

**Describe your comrades, and tell me what sort of people they are.**

"There's one comrade who grew up under the same blanket with me; he gave me fifty rubles when I was sick, so I think he's a good fellow and don't see any bad qualities in him. Generally I don't talk to bad people or become friendly with them; I'm a good buddy and have good buddies. I don't talk to people who play cards for money."

*Evaluates characteristics of comrades on basis of situation.*

**If someone was to be elected at a meeting, what person would you elect?**

"If my opinion was to be taken, I would choose someone who knew the work himself, had worked, and was poor."

Subject: Uzbaev., age forty, peasant from Uch-Kurgan, illiterate.

**Tell me the good features and shortcomings about your character.**

"I don't have enough wheat."

**No, tell me about your own traits, your character, your mind.**

"A good feature is that I don't talk to just anyone I come across; first I think how I will benefit from the conversation. If I will benefit, I begin to talk; if I see that there may be harm from it, I don't . . . I always choose my comrades. I think that this is a good trait. If I'm sitting in the courtyard and the children break something, I laugh and don't get angry. Another good thing is that I never argue with my family or other people. If someone behaves badly, I don't get abusive, I behave as if nothing had happened. The other person understands and becomes ashamed. These are my bad traits: if you say two or three false words a day, that'll be twenty to twenty-five words. So over a week your words will never be completely true. Our life always involves some false words. For instance, I promised my wife that I would buy her a dress at the bazaar, but in fact I didn't. That's not good."

*Detailed analysis of own behavior and characteristics.*

Subject: Yusup., age sixty-four, activist from Yangi-Yul farm, illiterate.

**What good qualities and what shortcomings could you name in yourself?**

"I'm never sad . . . what should I tell you—about outward or inward shortcomings?"

*Distinction between inward and outward shortcomings.*

**About inward ones, of course.**

"I feel that I'm a good person; I've had three wives. One of them became old and she brought me a young one. The young one left me when I went away. She asked for a divorce, but I didn't give it. I gave her one when I returned, and I feel that that's a good quality . . . My shortcoming is that I have no place to live. My old wife went off and locked everything up. That's a shortcoming of hers; they've treated me badly!"

*Approaches self-evaluation through a description of behavior in concrete situation. Slips back to external needs.*

**What do you feel it's necessary to change or improve about yourself?**

"I would like to educate myself in the modern fashion, so that things will go smoothly and I'll live the way people do nowadays. I don't know what I should change about myself. If I'm working, I want the work to go well."

**Tell me about your friends and their good and bad aspects.**

"My friends are good in every way. I don't know any bad aspects; I don't have bad comrades. Generally I don't talk to bad people but deal only with good ones. If someone helps me, I help him. All my buddies are kolkhozniks, they work for the kolkhoz. That's good. Maybe they have shortcomings, but they don't come up in the farmwork."

**If you had to elect someone at a meeting, who would you choose?**

"I would choose someone who works well and doesn't cause injury to others but defends their interests."

Subject: Khodzhyar., age twenty-one, worker from Batrak farm, spent one year in school.

**If you were asked to describe your good traits and the shortcomings in your character, how would you do it?**

"I don't know what is good and bad about me . . . One good quality is that I finished school and am working. One bad quality is that I'm still not working enough and I'm not literate enough. That's a shortcoming, but I don't have others."

*Description of qualities restricted to work and education; does not slip back into evaluating external material shortages.*

**What shortcomings does your wife see in you?**

"I just got married; my wife still doesn't see any shortcomings."

**What shortcomings do your comrades see?**

"My comrades get angry at me when I do something wrong on the farm. They say, 'You're young, you need to learn.' "

*Evaluation of quality in terms of evaluation of behavior.*

**Describe your comrades, and tell me what their good and bad qualities are.**

"Well, take Kazynbaev, we all point out his shortcomings at meetings. A good quality of his is that he's become a policeman, but a shortcoming is that he allowed a bad man to escape."

The transcripts of this transitional group of subjects display features familiar from the first group, but also some new ones. Frequently the subjects continue to point to external material disadvantages instead of intrinsic psychological properties or, in starting to describe such properties, they readily slip back into describing external features. The description of behavior or of their living situation continues to predominate.

Nonetheless, these subjects are making a consistent beginning to single out features of their behavior and psychological properties (which they also approach through concrete behavioral acts and life situations), and are ceasing to take the term "shortcoming" to mean an external material disadvantage. A typical feature is that evaluations of inward properties begin to engage both observations of the behavior of others and evaluations of one's own behavior which the subjects receive in the course of social life through participation in collective farming, planning of work, and collective evaluation of successes and failures. This shaping role of involvement in common enterprises and of evaluations stemming from collective life means that the subjects begin to put together notions of behavioral norms with which they compare their own behavior. They come to form an image of the "ideal me," which begins to play a decisive part in the further development of their consciousness.

All these features are particularly prominent in the final group of subjects, which consisted primarily of kolkhoz activists and those young people who had had some formal education and were actively involved in collective social life. Constant involvements in economic planning, and evaluation of work problems and advantages and disadvantages, create conditions for fundamental shifts in the analysis of one's own intrinsic qualities.

We begin with transcripts in which the description of one's own psychological features is still frequently replaced by descriptions of social work, clearly expressing the changing ideology under whose influence their personalities are shaped. Then we consider some of the more conspicuous instances of an internal restructuring in the consciousness of our subjects.

Subject: Lukman., age twenty-five, activist collective worker from village of Uch-Kurgan.

**How would you describe your character? Try to tell me your good features and shortcomings.**

"I have both my good sides and my shortcomings. I don't like to deal with mullahs, ishans [clergymen], or bais; I prefer to have to do with the poorest people or young children, even if they are badly dressed. I've seen my share of difficulties in life; my father was a farmhand. Although I didn't come into contact with the landowners, I don't like them. If I have to deal with landowners or mullahs, I don't refuse only so I can take from them what I need or find useful. My good side is that I don't like people who lie. If someone who lies to me is a worker, I explain to him that he can't do it. If he's not a worker, I refuse to speak to him and leave. I've been engaged in socialized work, and have drawn many of my comrades into the collective farm."

*Description of own social life and work.*

**You have told me about your social work. Now tell me the qualities that you yourself have, what your character is like, and what sort of a person you are.**

"My good traits are that I always try to acquire knowledge. I try to find out about everything, and my comrades ask me about things. I don't want to gain any advantage for myself, I do everything for others."

*Norms of social behavior.*

**And what are your negative features?**

"If somebody tries to do me a bad turn, I don't want to see them anymore, I don't want to take up work with them again . . . I can't get up enough enthusiasm, and when I'm asked to do something and it doesn't turn out, I don't pursue it; I don't feel like doing it. Why is this the case? I've lifted many baskets full of cookies; perhaps my brain was damaged as a result, or is it from lack of knowledge?"

*Goes from own shortcomings to those of other people; attempts to formulate own shortcomings.*

**What can you tell me about your personal qualities, your memory, character, will, quick-wittedness?**

"If someone gets into an argument and complains, I take both sides, first I learn everything in detail, I set up a commission, I don't jump to conclusions. That's the positive side of my actions."

*Evaluation of own qualities replaced by description of social behavior.*

**Now describe your comrades, their character, and their good features and shortcomings.**

"Well, take Sattarov. His bad qualities are that he likes money. If he's sent somewhere, instead of doing what needs to be done, he gets into a fight and a big ruckus follows. And then, he eavesdrops on conversations and passes them on . . . He doesn't distinguish between friends and enemies, but tells everything indiscriminately."

*Evaluation of psychological properties replaced by evaluation of social qualities.*

**Does he have good qualities?**

"I've lived here a long time, but I haven't seen them yet. There's just one thing. If he's told to do something, he won't refuse and is always involved in tasks. And then there's Khachkulov . . . First the good sides: he's very good about fulfilling obligations and is better than the rest at spadework. If a meeting is arranged, he won't refuse; he changes clothes and takes part. His attitude toward others is very good; he's never rude. If there are shortcomings in his work and they are pointed out to him, he doesn't get angry but tries to fix them . . . His bad qualities are that if a meeting judges his work and decides to reassign him, he won't admit what he's done and behaves like an innocent, and then talks to each one separately and tries to persuade them that they can't drop him, that he's a good person. He has a great deal of pride. He's something of a coward."

Here self-analysis involves external evaluations of one's own social work. The same analysis holds true of the psychological characteristics of other people. However, the range of qualities and situations engaged here in attempting to evaluate human positive and negative qualities differs radically from the references to material shortages and personal needs that comprised the content of "self-evaluation" for the subjects in the first group. Indeed, further observation showed that this is not the only mode of dealing with the task in question. There is also a more refined analysis of forms of behavior, gradually leading to an analysis of internal properties of personality.

Subject: Khaidar., age twenty-five, collective worker, barely literate.

**What has changed in you yourself of late?**

"Before I was a farmhand, I worked for a boss and didn't dare talk back to him; he did with me as he pleased. Now I know what my rights are."

**What shortcomings did you have before, and what ones do you have now?**

"Before I didn't know anything about freedom, and now I do. Before I worked a lot for others and couldn't get a pound of bread for my family, but on the farm I'm living better. I have things to give to others, and I even got married this year."

**But what changes have taken place in you yourself?**

"In me myself? Before I couldn't deal with anything, and now I'm managing somewhat, as you can see."

**What merits and shortcomings does a man have?**

"A man's merit is in how he deals with others. It's a shortcoming if he hasn't studied; if he studies, he will become a good person. If he studies, he will no longer deal badly with others."

**But are there good and bad people? What does this mean?**

"Well, if I had studied earlier and were literate, I wouldn't have had so much trouble; I would have known myself and my rights and would have been able to protect myself . . . If someone comes up to my sister and insults her, I answer him. If he's literate, he won't do it. But if he does, I don't act like a sissy, I'll also start abusing him, and that's my shortcoming."

**What sort of qualities do you think an intelligent man has?**

"If a man has studied since childhood and learns to write, we say that he has become an intelligent man. But if he doesn't learn, but just rides his donkey and sings songs, and knows nothing about where people come from, we say that he's a fool."

**Do an intelligent man and a fool have the same spirit?**

"No, it's different, of course. There are different people, like you and me—our spirit is different."

**In what way is it different?**

"You have your satisfactions, you study, you work, and I enjoy myself in my own way, so our spirit is different."

**And has your spirit changed as a result of the collective farm?**

"Of course it has . . . I've improved my work, I'm following a different path. I used to work for landowners and lived badly, but now I'm doing better on the farm."

**What qualities does the spirit have? Is memory, for instance, a quality of the spirit?**

"Yes, without memory there is no work; the memory shows what needs to be done, so people remember and work. The spirit controls this work. If you leave it to the spirit alone, it can't do anything by itself."

**And what other important human qualities are there?**

"There's a man's nature (*tabiet*). If your nature wants to do something, you know it; if it's against his nature, a man can't do anything . . . People also have imagination (*khaiol*), intelligence (*akyl*), thought (*fikir*), and spirit (*rokhe*)—all these combine and the result is work. If a man can't use his imagination, his attention (*khysh*) is not oriented to his work and he can't do it."

We have given this long excerpt to show how refined and complex the notions of mental properties can be, and what set of concepts we may encounter if we ask our subjects to evaluate their internal properties and those of others.

Subject: Tekan, age thirty-six, collective-farm activist.

**What good traits and what shortcomings do you know about yourself?**

"I'm neither good nor bad . . . I'm an average person, though I'm weak on literacy and can't write at all; and then I'm very nasty and angry, but still, I don't beat my wife. That's all I can say about myself . . . I forget very fast; I walk out of a room and I forget. I also don't understand very well; yesterday I was given a long explanation, and I didn't understand anything. If I were educated, I would do everything well. I have to change this shortcoming in education. I don't want to change anything in my character; if I study, it'll change by itself."

*Readily distinguishes psychological features.*

We have only to compare these transcripts with the refusals to distinguish psychological properties with which we began our description to discern the remarkable process of shaping of individual consciousness that has occurred within a relatively short historical period.

It is particularly important that this process is not exhausted merely by a shift in the content of consciousness and an opening up of new spheres of life (spheres of social experience and of relationships to oneself as a participant in social life) to conscious analysis. We are dealing with much more fundamental shifts—the formation of new psychological systems, capable of reflecting not only external reality but also the world of social relations and ultimately one's own inner world as shaped in relation to other people. This formation of a new inner world can be regarded as one of the fundamental achievements of the historical period under consideration.

In conclusion, we present Table 11, where the relationship between the changes we have described and the profound social shifts we could observe is particularly prominent.

Table 11.  Evaluation of One's Own Psychological Features

| Group | Refusal to analyze, reference to material conditions and situation | Transitional group | Analysis of psychological features |
|---|---|---|---|
| Illiterate peasants from remote villages (20 subjects) | 13 (65%) | 6 (30%) | 1 (5%) |
| Collective-farm workers who completed short-term program (15 subjects) | 0 | 13 (86%) | 2 (14%) |
| Young people with short-term education, farm activists (17 subjects) | 0 | 6 (35%) | 11 (65%) |

# 8

## Conclusion

We have considered certain data that show the changes in the structure
of mental processes associated with cognitive activity at different
stages of historical development, and the major shifts that have occurred in these processes under the impact of a social and cultural
revolution. The facts we obtained, which form a fragment of a more
extensive undertaking, yield certain major conclusions of great importance for understanding the nature and structure of human cognitive
processes. The facts show convincingly that the structure of cognitive
activity does not remain static during different stages of historical
development and that the most important forms of cognitive processes
—perception, generalization, deduction, reasoning, imagination, and
analysis of one's own inner life—vary as the conditions of social life
change and the rudiments of knowledge are mastered.

Our investigations, which were conducted under unique and non-
replicable conditions involving a transition to collectivized forms of
labor and cultural revolution, showed that, as the basic forms of
activity change, as literacy is mastered, and a new stage of social and
historical practice is reached, major shifts occur in human mental
activity. These are not limited simply to an expanding of man's
horizons, but involve the creation of new motives for action and radically affect the structure of cognitive processes.

A basic feature of the shifts we observed is that the role of direct graphic-functional experience was radically altered in the transition to collectivized labor and new forms of social relations and with the mastery of rudiments of theoretical knowledge.

In addition to elementary graphic-functional motives, we see the creation of new motives that take shape in the process of collectivized labor, the joint planning of labor activity, and basic schooling. These complex motives, which go beyond concrete practical activity, assume the form of conscious planning of one's own labor; we begin to see interests that go beyond immediate impressions and the reproduction of concrete forms of practical activity. These motives include future planning, the interests of the collective, and, finally, a number of important cultural topics that are closely associated with achievement of literacy and assimilation of theoretical knowledge.

Closely associated with this assimilation of new spheres of social experience, there are dramatic shifts in the nature of cognitive activity and the structure of mental processes. The basic forms of cognitive activity begin to go beyond fixation and reproduction of individual practical activity and cease to be purely concrete and situational. Human cognitive activity becomes a part of the more extensive system of general human experience as it has become established in the process of social history, coded in language.

Perception begins to go beyond graphic, object-oriented experience and incorporates much more complex processes which combine what is perceived into a system of abstract, linguistic categories. Even the perception of colors and shapes changes, becoming a process in which direct impressions are related to complex abstract categories.

The generalized way in which reality is reflected also undergoes radical restructuring. The isolation of the essential features of objects and the assignment of objects to a general category of objects with the same features ceases to be regarded as something minor and insignificant. New, theoretical thought operations arise—analysis of the properties of things, assignment of them to abstract categories, and so forth. Thinking processes begin to involve more and more abstraction and generalization. Theoretical, "categorical" thought begins to function in addition to operations of practical "situational" thinking and occupies a more prominent place, sometimes beginning to dominate human cognitive activity. Gradually we see the "transition from the sensory to the rational'' which modern materialistic philosophy, as we have noted, tends to regard as one of the most important aspects of the development of consciousness.

Together with new forms of abstract, categorical relationships to reality, we also see the appearance of new forms of mental dynamics. Whereas before the dynamics of thought occurred only within the framework of immediate, practical experience and reasoning processes were largely limited to processes of reproducing established practical situations, as a result of the cultural revolution we see the possibility of drawing inferences not only on the basis of one's own practical experience, but on the basis of discursive, verbal, and logical processes as well.

It becomes possible to take assumptions as they are formulated in language and use them to make logical inferences, regardless of whether or not the content of the premise forms a part of personal experience. The relationship to logical reasoning that goes beyond immediate experience is radically restructured; we see the creation of the rudiments of discursive thinking, whose inferences become as compelling as those from direct, personal experience.

All these transformations result in changes in the basic structure of cognitive processes and result in an enormous expansion of experience and in the construction of a vastly broader world in which human beings begin to live. In addition to the sphere of personal experience, we see the appearance of the sphere of abstract general human experience as established in language and in the operations of discursive thinking. Human thought begins to rest on broad logical reasoning; the sphere of creative imagination takes shape, and this in turn vastly expands man's subjective world.

Finally, there are changes in self-awareness of the personality, which advances to the higher level of social awareness and assumes new capabilities for objective, categorical analysis of one's motivation, actions, intrinsic properties, and idiosyncracies. Thus a fact hitherto underrated by psychology becomes apparent: sociohistorical shifts not only introduce new content into the mental world of human beings; they also create new forms of activity and new structures of cognitive functioning. They advance human consciousness to new levels.

We see now the inaccuracy of the centuries-old notions in accordance with which the basic structures of perception, representation, reasoning, deduction, imagination, and self-awareness are fixed forms of spiritual life and remain unchanged under differing social conditions. The basic categories of human mental life can be understood as products of social history—they are subject to change when the basic forms of social practice are altered and thus are social in nature.

Psychology comes primarily to mean the science of the sociohistorical shaping of mental activity and of the structures of mental processes which depend utterly on the basic forms of social practice and the major stages in the historical development of society. The basic theses of Marxism regarding the historical nature of human mental life are thus revealed in their concrete forms. This becomes possible as a result of the radical, revolutionary shifts permitting us to observe, over a brief period, fundamental changes which under ordinary conditions would require centuries.

Scholars who took upon themselves the task of examining our work as it was being prepared frequently expressed the wish that we carry out the same research again in order to make a comparative analysis of the further changes that have occurred over the past forty years in these locations. While this suggestion is quite reasonable, we do not feel compelled to follow it.

Our data show what major changes in the structure of cognitive processes began to take place during the period of our original research, shifts that had already taken place in the first years of the cultural revolution for the inhabitants of the remoter parts of our country. Since then, the author has repeatedly been to Uzbekistan and has witnessed the enormous changes in social and cultural life that have occurred during these years. To repeat, the research in the same localities forty years later, during which time the peoples of central Asia have, in effect, made a leap of centuries, would be superfluous. An investigator who desired to replicate our work would obtain data that differ little from those he might obtain by studying the structure of cognitive processes among inhabitants in any other part of the Soviet Union.

In the past forty years, a backward and remote region has become an economically and socially developed part of our socialist state, and the author can only express his complete satisfaction that, together with his group of comrades, he was able to make his observations at a time when these shifts had only just begun.

Bibliography

Index

# Bibliography

Ach, N. *Über die Willenstätigkeit und das Denken*. Göttingen: Vandenhoeck and Ruprecht, 1905.

Allen, G. *The colour-sense: Its origin and development*. Boston: Houghton, Osgood, 1879.

Allport, G. W., and T. F. Pettigrew. Cultural influence on the perception of movement: The trapezoidal illusion among Zulus. *Journal of Abnormal and Social Psychology*, 1957, *55*, 104-113.

Beveridge, W. M. Racial differences in phenomenal regression. *British Journal of Psychology*, 1935, *26*, 59-62.

_____ Some racial differences in perception. *British Journal of Psychology*, 1939, *30*, 57-64.

Blondel, C. *La mentalité primitive*. Paris: Stock, 1926.

Boas, F. *The mind of primitive man*. New York: Macmillan, 1911.

Brown, R. W., and E. H. Lenneberg. A study in language and cognition. *Journal of Abnormal and Social Psychology*, 1954, *59*, 454-462.

Bruner, J. S. Going beyond the information given. In *Contemporary approaches to cognition: A symposium held at the University of Colorado*. Cambridge: Harvard University Press, 1957.

Brunswick, E., and J. Kamiya. Ecological cue-validation of "proximity" and other Gestalt factors. *American Journal of Psychology*, 1953, *66*, 20-32.

Conklin, H. C. Hanunoo color categories. *Southwestern Journal of Anthropology*, 1955, *11*, 339-344.

Deregowski, J. B. Difficulties in pictorial depth perception in Africa. *British Journal of Psychology*, 1968, *59*, 195-204.

_____ On perception of depicted orientation. *International Journal of Psychology*, 1968, *3*, 149-156.

Durkheim, E., and M. Mauss. *Primitive classification*. Chicago: University of Chicago Press, 1963.

Eccles, J. C. *Facing reality: Philosophical adventures by a brain scientist*. Heidelberg Science Library, vol. 13. New York: Springer-Verlag, 1970.

Elkonin, D. B. *Child psychology*. Moscow: 1960 (in Russian).

Galperin, P. Y. The mental act as the basis for the formation of ideas and images. *Problems of Psychology,* 1957, *6*.

Goldstein, K. *Language and language disturbances*. New York: Grune and Stratton, 1948.

Gurgenidze, G. S., and A. R. Luria. Philosophical adventures of an outstanding physiologist. *Voprosy filosofii,* 1972, *3*.

Hallowell, A. I. Cultural factors in the structuralization of perception. In *Conference on social psychology at the cross-roads,* ed. J. H. Rohrer and M. Sherif. New York: Harper, 1951.

_____ *Culture and experience*. Philadelphia: University of Pennsylvania Press, 1955.

Hoijer, H., ed. Language in culture: Conference on the interrelations of language and other aspects of culture. Chicago: University of Chicago Press, 1954.

Hunt, E. B. *Concept learning*. New York: Wiley, 1962.

Lenneberg, E. H., and D. Roberts. *The language of experience*. Memoir 13, Indiana University Publications in Anthropology and Linguistics, supplement to *International Journal of American Linguistics,* vol. 22. Baltimore: Waverly Press, 1956.

Leroy, O. *La raison primitive*. Paris: Geuthner, 1927.

Lévi-Strauss, C. Social structure. In *Anthropology Today,* ed. A. L. Kroeber. Chicago: University of Chicago Press, 1953.

Lévy-Bruhl, L. *Primitive mentality*. New York: Macmillan, 1923.

Lindsay, P. H., and D. A. Norman. *Human information processing: An introduction to psychology*. New York: Academic Press, 1972.

Luria, A. R. "The brain and conscious experience": A critical notice of the symposium edited by J. C. Eccles (1966). *British Journal of Philosophy,* 1967, *58,* 467-476.

_____ and L. S. Tsvetkova. *Neuropsychological analysis of problem-solving*. Moscow: 1966 (in Russian).

Magnus, H. *Die geschichtliche Entwicklung des Farbensinnes*. Leipzig: 1877.

_____ *Über ethnologische Untersuchungen des Farbensinnes*. Berlin: 1883.

_____ *Untersuchungen über den Farbensinn der Naturvölker*. Jena: 1880.

Ray, V. F. Techniques and problems in the study of human color perception. *Southwestern Journal of Anthropology,* 1952, *8,* 251-259.

Rivers, W. H. R. Primitive color vision. *Popular Science Monthly,* 1901, *59,* 44-58.

_____ Observations on the sense of the Todas. *British Journal of Psychology,* 1905, *1,* 321-396.

_____ *Psychology and ethnology*. New York: Harcourt, Brace, 1926.

Segall, M. H., D. T. Campbell, and M. J. Herskovits. *The influence of culture on visual perception.* Indianapolis: Bobbs-Merrill, 1966.

Tylor, E. B. *Primitive culture.* London: J. Murray, 1891.

Virchow, R. Über die Nubier. *Zeitschrift für Ethnologie,* 1878, *10*; 1879, *11*.

Vygotsky, L. S. *Thought and language.* Cambridge: Massachusetts Institute of Technology Press, 1962.

Whorf, B. L. *Language, thought and reality.* Cambridge: Massachusetts Institute of Technology Press, 1956.

Woodworth, R. S. Color sense in different races of mankind. *Proceedings of the Society for Experimental Biology and Medicine,* 1905-1906, *3.*

Yarbus, A. L. *Eye movements and vision.* New York: Plenum, 1967.

Zaporozhets, A. V. *Development of voluntary movement in children.* Moscow: 1960 (in Russian).

# Index